It's You!

Also by Emily Cho

Looking Terrific
(with Linda Grover)

Looking, Working, Living Terrific 24 Hours a Day
(with Hermine Lueders)

EMILY CHO

And Neila Fisher with Hermine Lueders

It's You!

Looking Terrific Whatever Your Type

Illustrations by Cheryl Lickona

Minimal wardrobe illustrations by Neila Fisher

BALLANTINE BOOKS · NEW YORK

Copyright © 1986 by Emily Cho and
Hermine Lueders

All rights reserved under International and
Pan-American Copyright Conventions. Published
in the United States by Ballantine Books, a divi-
sion of Random House, Inc., New York, and
simultaneously in Canada by Random House
of Canada Limited, Toronto.

Library of Congress Catalog Card Number:
86-91562

ISBN: 0-345-33164-8

This edition published by arrangement with
Villard Books.

Cover design by James R. Harris
Photo by Anthony Lowe

Manufactured in the United States of America

First Ballantine Books Edition: April 1987

10 9 8 7 6 5 4 3 2 1

To Julie and Lucy . . .

With the hope that they will discover for
themselves the very special joys of giving
their individuality its fullest expression.

ACKNOWLEDGMENTS

Neila and I need to thank the two people who turned our idea into a reality by understanding exactly what we were trying to say and presenting it as we conceived it. Our warmest thanks to

Hermine, whose remarkable ability to translate free-flowing thoughts into organized concepts enabled us to get across to you a very complex subject.

Cheryl, who worked so long and hard on every detail of each image-type that they came alive for us all. Without her willingness to change and change again the minor details of each illustration, this book would not have been as accurate as it is.

If you would like information on private services provided, or on the professional image-consultant course, write:

Emily Cho Inc.
14 E. 90th Street
New York, NY 10128

CONTENTS

4

If You're an Exotic-Dramatic   68

Seeing yourself as others see you

How to change how others see you

Basic and Creative dressing unlimited—from image-type to the individual you are

5

If You're an Arty-Offbeat   92

Seeing yourself as others see you

How to change how others see you

Basic and Creative dressing unlimited—from image-type to the individual you are

6

If You're a Feminine-Romantic   116

Seeing yourself as others see you

How to change how others see you

Basic and Creative dressing unlimited—from image-type to the individual you are

7

If You're a Sexy-Alluring   138

Seeing yourself as others see you

How to change how others see you

Basic and Creative dressing unlimited—from image-type to the individual you are

8

Crossover Dressing   162

9

Conclusion   184

Every Image-Type Is Exciting

It's You!

1

INTRODUCTION

The aim of this book is very simple: to take the fear out of fashion—and put in the fun.

Never has image been such an important part of our lives. Never have image and fashion been so much in the public eye—and in the public consciousness. You can't open a magazine, flip through a newspaper, turn on the TV without seeing something about fashion. Who's wearing it, who's creating it, who's critiquing it; what's out, what's in; and where it's all going next.

Watching the who, what, and where of it can be fun. It's when you get to the "how" that so many of us feel the fun ebbing and the fear flowing in. So much seems to ride on being savvy about fashion—the career you break into, the men you attract, how good you feel about yourself. Yet the rules change so fast, and there's so much conflicting advice, it's hard to know when you're on the right track and when you're not.

It doesn't have to be that hard, or that iffy, or even that complicated. By the time you finish this book, you'll agree.

The secret of dressing well is much the same as the secret of doing anything well: Know what you're doing and why you're doing it. In other words, *following the rules.*

The secret of dressing superbly well—individually, strikingly, joyously well—is knowing when and how to break the rules. However, you can't get there by taking shortcuts. You really do have to understand the rules first. People who don't take the time and effort to do that may think they're free spirits, but all too often they look *lost*, like people who don't know what they're doing or who they are; they have no idea how they really look to the world. As a result, life is much harder for them.

If we were all born alike, fashion could be reduced to mathematics: two plus two equals four. Take a black suit, add a white blouse, and you're dressed for business—no matter who you are or what your business is. But we all know life isn't that simple—and a good thing, too, because where would all the fun go? The fact is, we're not all alike, each of us is an individual, and expressing our individuality is one of the real highs of living. Indeed, getting to know who you really are is the main joy of maturing.

The real challenge is how do you and where do you start to define your individuality? The surest way is to start with the six essential image-types and discover which one you feel yourself to be. Are you a Classic-Elegant or an Arty-Offbeat? A Sporty-Casual or a Sexy-Alluring? A Feminine-Romantic or an Exotic-Dramatic?

When you've made your choice, you've found that starting place, the core of you. It may be a core you share with many others, but it is a basic step in defining your individuality. When creating the face or figure of a woman, an artist first decides on the basic characteristics—the shape of the face, the proportions of the figure—before filling in the specifics: the eyes, the nose, the mouth, the breasts, that make each woman individual. Our six types serve the same purpose.

"But," you say, "what if I don't want to be categorized as one image-type." Suppose you feel you're being shoehorned into something that won't feel like a perfect fit because it doesn't express all of you.

Don't worry. Finding your image-type will not restrict you, it will *free* you. Most of our clients don't want an endless amount of choice, they want a solution that simplifies their lives.

That's exactly what defining your image-type does for you. It doesn't leave you lost and wandering in the pages of the fashion magazines or poking through the department stores and boutiques trying to find *your* dress or jacket or blouse out of the avalanche of new styles that come out each spring and fall. When you've sorted out your image, you've already sorted out the kind of clothes you're looking for, before you've even stepped inside the store. And that's the biggest time-, money-, and energy-saver of all. Even better, it's the surest way to look your best.

The Six Main Image-Types:
Which One Are You?

Not exactly sure which image-type you are? Find out now. Answer the ten questions that follow, take the Visual Quiz—and you'll see. Just select and add up how many of each letter you have.

Quiz

1. If you could be born again, who would you most like to look like?
   A. Christie Brinkley
   B. Jackie Onassis
   C. Diana Ross
   D. Diane Keaton
   E. Jane Seymour
   F. Raquel Welch

2. Which kind of makeup makes it for you?
   A. No makeup
   B. Understatedly perfect
   C. Highly dramatic
   D. Very à la mood
   E. Palest possible
   F. Vibrant and glossy

3. Assuming your hair would cooperate, what style would you choose?
   A. Short casual cut
   B. Shoulder-length blunt cut swinging hair
   C. Hair sleekly pulled back away from your face
   D. Frizzed hair
   E. Long, wavy hair
   F. Full, softly layered hair

4. If your body could wear it, which would your soul be happiest in?
   A. Crisp cotton camp shirt and pants
   B. Ivory wool gabardine suit
   C. Slim shift of magenta hammered satin with big shoulders, skinny push-up sleeves, narrow short skirt
   D. Narrow leather pants and oversized blazer
   E. White Victorian lace summer dress
   F. Red sequin mini-dress

5. What would you wear to a large cocktail party to make a "knock-out" impression?
   A. Colorful silk blouse and black skirt
   B. Simple black dress
   C. Evening tunic over black pants
   D. 1940s print dress
   E. Mauve silk dress
   F. Low-cut electric blue dress

6. Which texture turns you to jelly at a touch?
   A. Soft tweed
   B. Silk
   C. Thin, fine suede
   D. Antique cut-velvet
   E. Angora
   F. Satin

7. Which is the one piece of jewelry you'd feel naked without?
   A. A gold chain necklace
   B. A Cartier watch
   C. A strong brass or pewter choker
   D. An Art Deco belt
   E. An old cameo pin
   F. Diamond drop earrings

8. Which kind of colors color you happy?
   A. Primaries
   B. Pale neutrals
   C. Black
   D. Offbeat, neons
   E. Soft pastels
   F. Electric red and electric blue

9. Assuming your shape is no problem, which clothing shapes are you most drawn to?
   A. Crisp and linear
   B. Sleek and defined
   C. Angular and asymmetric
   D. Oversized and unconventional
   E. Soft and flowing
   F. Body-hugging

10. Which compliment would delight you the most?
    A. "You're so much fun to be with."
    B. "You have such elegant taste."
    C. "You have fantastic style."
    D. "You're so *creative*."
    E. "You look like a dream!"
    F. "You're always a knockout!"

Visual Quiz

Which jacket?

A

B

C

Which dress?

A

B

C

"Which One Are You?"

D   E   F

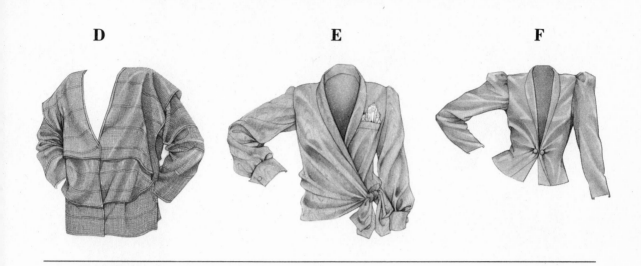

D   E   F

Visual Quiz

Which black tie outfit?

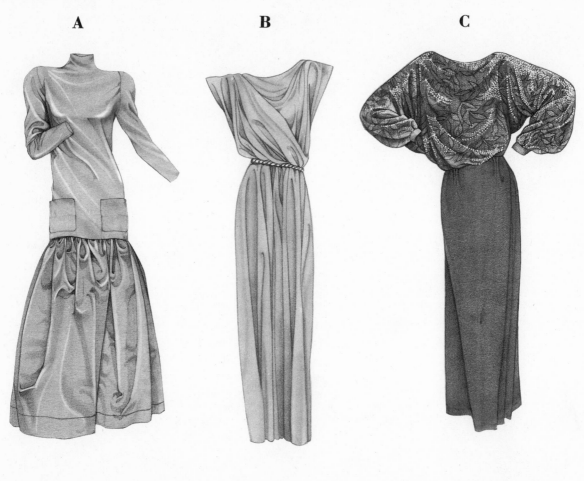

A   B   C

Scoring

If you have seven or more A's, you're a Sporty-Casual; seven or more B's, a Classic-Elegant; seven or more C's, Exotic-Dramatic; seven or more D's, Arty-Offbeat; seven or more E's, Feminine-Romantic; seven or more F's, Sexy-Alluring.

"Which One Are You?"

D   E   F

If your score divides more or less evenly among several letters—for example, six A's, four B's, three C's—you're the image-type of the letter that scored highest, with a greater than average potential for crossing over into another image-type from time to time. (There's a whole chapter on crossovers that will tell you how and when.)

Once you've figured out your image-type, you're ready to take the second step: to embellish and define your individuality within that type.

This two-step process makes everything easier for you—and for the world. Finding your image helps you identify yourself to the world, and helps the world get a handle on you. Dressing to achieve this first step is what we call Basic dressing. It tells the world what *kind* of person you are—but it doesn't go further and say this is the *specific* person you are. Creative dressing says that.

You'll be finding out more and more about Basic and Creative dressing throughout this book. (Not only the how-to but the why-, when-, and where-to.) Right now, let's just say it starts with defining your image parameters. In the pages ahead, image parameters figure almost as importantly as image-types. That's to make sure you take advantage of all the flexibility every image can provide. It's easy to think of an image-type as a single, fixed entity, but if you do, you can feel trapped. An image-type is not a dot on a map, it's an *area,* a surprisingly wide area, even if it's within boundaries. When you think in terms of your image parameters, your field of operations is enormously widened. (Or, to put it a little less formally, you've got a lot more room in which to play and, better yet, in which to play with confidence.)

If your type is Classic-Elegant and you are a Basic dresser within the category, you can't go over the edge . . . can't go wrong in any way. You won't be sending confusing signals about what kind of person you are. You'll be sending a true message about yourself but you won't be revealing anything really *personal.* Basic dressing, for any of the six main types, is conservative, because it's always true, honest, and typical of that type.

Generally speaking, for all the six types, Basic dressing consists of what is expected for that type, choosing the more tailored silhouette, the more precise line. Creative dressing is dressing with more flair, choosing the looser silhouette, the softer line.

Basic is conforming to the basic image, striking close to its center. Creative is giving your own personality more play, reaching out to the far ends of the image. Basic is the safe, more conventional route, less experimental, less individual. Creative is more confident, more daring, in keeping with this era of self-assurance and ease.

Making a distinction between Basic and Creative dressing is not meant to imply that one is better than the other. Rather, the intention is to open your eyes to the range of options you have to choose from within your type. Basic and Creative make it possible to be two good things at once: true-to-type and individual.

Best of all, Basic and Creative don't necessarily call for two different wardrobes. They are sometimes distinguished by nothing more than a matter of small details, or different accessories, or even *how* something is worn.

A few examples:

Basic Sporty is a lined, structured blazer.
Creative Sporty is an unlined, unconstructed jacket.

Basic Classic is a tailored skirt or pleated pants.
Creative Classic is a culotte skirt or cropped pants.

Basic Exotic is one strong accessory as a signature piece.
Creative Exotic is a starkly simple, offbeat dress, totally unadorned.

Basic Arty is high leather boots.
Creative Arty is layers of colorful, patterned legwarmers.

Basic Feminine is an angora turtleneck sweater.
Creative Feminine is a V-neck open-weave cotton sweater.

Basic Sexy is a short, tight mini-skirt.
Creative Sexy is a longer straight skirt with side slits.

These are only examples to give you the idea. In the pages ahead you'll see how the range between Basic and Creative can open up a limitless field of experimentation for you. You can slide easily from Basic to Creative within your image. We'll show you how you can start Basic (and stay Basic if you want) and experiment with Creative when the mood hits, when the occasion is different, when you want to give people a little surprise, or when you see a fabulous buy you can't pass up. The more you experiment, the more your self-confidence grows, the freer you feel, the less you'll worry about making mistakes. Then you'll be ready for even wider fields of experiment—that is, Crossover dressing.

What's Crossover dressing? It's the answer to a problem many women have without being able to describe it exactly: what to do if you're not a "pure" type.

If you feel there are facets of you that seem to come from one or two of the other types, that's not a mistake—that's real life. The types described here should more accurately be thought of as *archetypes*—the purest form of each type, deliberately described that way, to make it easier to compare and contrast and identify them.

Real live women are not "pure" abstractions, not one-dimensional. They want and need the flexibility—and fun—of dressing their whole selves, which may include certain characteristics of other types. That's Crossover dressing—and it's a vitally important part of this whole book. Crossovers give every woman, no matter what her particular type, a chance to use the strengths of other types to her own advantage. Later you'll see just how it's done—and how exhilarating it can be. Indeed, for the very sophisticated woman, Crossover dressing is the deliberate and calculated borrowing from any of the other types to gain a psychological edge in a given situation.

If you're a Sporty-Casual, and you've just met the man of your dreams, how do you cross over into Feminine-Romantic without losing your own identity? Or if you're an Arty-Offbeat, how do you cross over into Classic-Elegant for that crucial job interview without looking as if you're putting on an act? The problems—and the opportunities—are endless, and the outcomes often so important, that Crossover dressing can provide the edge that makes all the difference.

Here it's enough to say that using crossovers effectively is graduate-level dressing. You've finished your basic clothing education. You've learned so much, so well, you feel sure enough of yourself to strike out in other areas. You "cross over" to other image-types for any number of reasons. Not by accident, not by mistake, not because of ignorance, but because you know exactly what you're doing and why. Because your lifestyle has changed or your job has changed or you've moved to another part of the country. Or because your ideas have changed, you're hungry for a little adventure, a little chance-taking, a little experimentation on a wider scale in a lot of directions.

But mainly because *you've* changed. You're aware of sides of your personality you didn't even know before. You want to see what happens when you let the world see them. You want to feel the difference it makes to your self-image when you recognize them and let them have free play. How much more of a person you feel yourself to be—because you're more intriguing, more aware, more able to be *all the things you are.*

Suddenly you realize you're having fun. Not the fun of a child splashing around in the water, kicking her feet every which way, not knowing what she's doing, but the fun of a first-class swimmer, cutting through the surf with effortless ease; because she knows the strokes so well, she doesn't even have to think about them——they're as natural and easy as breathing. It's the kind of pleasure that will last a lifetime because you'll continually enjoy good feedback. That's the kind of pleasure clothes should——and can——give every woman. And the whole aim of this book is to help you prove it to yourself.

The section for each image-type delineates the profile of that type and details Basic and Creative dressing for all the categories in one's job, home, and social life. The ideal minimal wardrobe, colors, textures, and accessories are also discussed. For a better understanding of your own image-type, also read the other image-types. You'll see how you compare with others in each arena of life. Then see how wide a world opens up to you in the last chapter as you learn how to borrow from other image-types, to draw out different responses from people, and achieve the better results you want in your life.

Sporty-Casual   *Classic-Elegant*   *Exotic-Dramatic*

Arty-Offbeat   *Feminine-Romantic*   *Sexy-Alluring*

2

If You're a

SPORTY-CASUAL

If you scored more A's than any other letter, on both the Questionnaire and the Visual Quiz, you're the Sporty-Casual type and you're in good company.

Sally Field	*Stefanie Powers*
Mariel Hemingway	*Christie Brinkley*
Cheryl Tiegs	*Farrah Fawcett*
Jane Fonda	*Ali MacGraw*
Dinah Shore	*Mary Tyler Moore*

As you can tell from the list of names, the Sporty-Casual is the quintessential "American Girl" image famous the world over. A perennial favorite for decades, the Sporty-Casual comes in all ages, sizes, hairstyles and hair colors, face shapes, and skin tones. Yet underlying all the surface variety are certain common basics—in personality, life-style, attitude toward clothes, and beauty—basics you undoubtedly share.

The common thread is *energy*. If you're a Sporty-Casual, energy is as basic to you as breathing. Everything you enjoy, everything you care about involves energy in some form—discharging it, recharging it, and above all reveling in it.

Whether you're at home or on the job, your day is much more likely to be "up-and-at-'em" than "let's-sit-down-and-think-this-out." If you're running errands, touching bases, covering ground, in and out of cars and cabs, you want your clothes to be able to keep up with you. Comfort is of the essence. So is easy upkeep. Hence no tight necklines or waistbands. No fabrics that wrinkle the minute you sit down. No colors that soil on first wearing. You'd rather have A-line skirts—straight skirts are too constricting, full skirts too cumbersome. You lean toward tailored clothes rather than frilly, the conservative rather than the latest fad.

When it comes to social life, you'd have more fun at a casual party than at a formal dance. Your formal occasions are usually annual events with a familiar crowd. For those, you usually resort to a long skirt and a colorful silk blouse.

For you, cleanliness is the essence of beauty. You insist on wash-and-wear hair. As long as it's clean and healthy—and you don't have to fuss with it—you're happy. Not for you all the curling and shaping, spraying and coloring; you've had an easy-care cut for years.

Others think there's a lot to like about you. You're natural and unpretentious. People know they can always count on those generous reserves of energy you have on tap, that spirited "let's do it" approach to life. People feel that what they know about you is what you *are* (an especially endearing quality in these days when there are so many impostors around).

If you're not careful, however, you can be seen as a little too conservative, trim, safe most of the time. Too regular with no surprises. It's an easy mistake to make if you haven't developed a philosophy about clothes and image. You've been stalled in casualness and comfort for so long, your clothes are first and foremost practical. Cotton instead of silk, khaki instead of white, solid colors instead of prints. You think you should look as if very little effort went into getting your "look" together, with just the bare minimum of accessorizing—maybe just a narrow, classic belt.

What are the pitfalls of your image? Chances are you've got the day-time sporty look down pat. It's who you are as a female in the evenings that is the problem. That's where you have the most trouble getting your image right, because it never feels like *you*. You always feel you're dressed up in someone else's clothes. Usually the problem is that you just don't change enough. You still can't get the makeup on to quite the right effect . . . in a way that signals "evening." And so, even though you change into a pretty colorful silk dress, it still looks wrong because it doesn't have the support of the right makeup, hair, and accessories.

Or you make the opposite mistake and put on too much makeup or the wrong shade of a clear eyeshadow—blue, turquoise, or green.

The pluses of your image are readily apparent. *Your* look is just about the easiest to get together because America's life-style is so sports-oriented, casual, and easygoing. The market is flooded with your choice of clothes. Your day look can run the gamut from safari to tweedy Prep to strong primary-color combinations.

As it is, your clothing hangups are easy to spot. They show up not only in your closet, but in your seasonal shopping patterns. And what they say is, you're a little shy about revealing your femininity and the role it plays in your life. You've never thought of yourself as pretty—or *not* pretty, for that matter. Just active. (Which is not at all a bad thing to be; it's just not enough, when you could be so much more.)

The wardrobe in your closet probably adds up like this:

Colors and Combinations	Mostly beige and brown (instead of black or taupe)
	Primary colors: clear and usually solid (you wouldn't think of wearing two or more together)
Patterns	Subtle geometrics: glen plaids, small checks, stripes (no polka dots—too Marilyn Monroe)
Florals	If at all, they're small (never in a dramatic print that draws a lot of attention)
Textures	Flat and smooth, even when it comes to tweeds (thick and nubby might be too complicated to cope with—or live up to)
Accessories	Too little, too plain, too few (a classic gold and silver ring, a gold chain or two; small gold hoop or stud earrings; a leather belt)
	For summer: earrings and necklace of wood, and a rope belt.
	And always in "sets"—pearl earrings with a pearl necklace (for an important function, always your "important set")

And your seasonal shopping patterns? In keeping with the above: safe and same. Also, as much as possible, fast and easy.

Safe and Same	One put-together outfit in September, another in April for spring (each usually in the same color family as the one you've always had)
Fast and Easy	Each season you make a beeline for the same store—and the same department in that store (you like to feel you're being smart and efficient—you'd hate to think you might be scared and lazy)

As for seasonal updates, they never cross your mind. You think you use up enough energy just getting the one or two outfits you manage to put together each season.

To sum it all up: Just what does Sporty-Casual add up to? On the positive side: natural, energetic, easy to be with, practical, high-spirited, and dependable. On the negative side, safe, predictable, unadventurous, and just a teensy bit lazy when it comes to bestirring yourself to make the most of yourself.

Sporty-Casuals have been known to wish, at times, they were some other type. Yet never were the times better for a particular image-type than today is for the Sporty-Casual. The very definition of beauty has changed, and it's now all about you. The heart of it is energy—your very essence. With your energy, and all the rest you've got going for you—attributes every woman wants—it's worth your while as never before to make the most of all you have. And once you start to see the results of even the smallest changes, you'll wonder why you ever wished to be anybody else. You yourself can be terrific!

Clothes for the Sporty-Casual

Basic and Creative

Note: As you study the illustrations in the following pages it's important to keep in mind that Basic means essentially "expected" for that type, and Creative means a looser, "less-expected" interpretation.

For the Sporty-Casual, the "expected" is easy skirts, blazer jackets,

A-line silhouettes, practical fabrics, basic colors, a generally comfortable, dressed-down look.

The looser, "less-expected" interpretation would consist of straight skirts, unstructured jackets, more fluid lines, easier silhouettes, softer fabrics, and a casual but more put-together look.

Dressing for Your Job

As a Sporty-Casual, you have one great advantage: you don't look as if you put your clothes ahead of your job. You look ready to roll up your sleeves, plunge right in, and concentrate on what needs doing. But that first-things-first attitude can backfire. You may look as if you just put on any old shirt and skirt—and forgot your belt, or didn't bother with accessories. "Casual" can veer into "sloppy" if you're not careful.

But even when you're wrong, you never look inappropriate for work, probably just somewhat underdressed (and on the job, that's better than being overdressed). While that kind of underdressing may not help in other aspects of your life, on the job it doesn't hurt. It's possible that you may be considered for more job opportunities because of your casual easygoing presentation of yourself.

You, more than any other type, can afford to "dress up" for your job. When you change to higher heels, put on a jacket for client meetings, wear a tailored red blouse, and finish with just a few accessories, you show your boss and your co-workers that you understand the importance of the occasion. No more, no less. It's self-respect, as well as respect for others, to make the effort.

The fact is, when you dress appropriately for the person you are and for your job, it's the best way to get to the place you want to be. Throughout the book, Basic and Creative examples for three different job levels will help you find the right look for your work wardrobe.

Dressing for Your Home Life

For you, dressing for home is the most fun of all because you can forget about clothes and just be yourself. But think about that for a minute. Is it really "fun"—or just relief because you don't have to worry and wonder and plan? Then think about what that relief may be costing you.

If you spend too many of your waking hours in rock-bottom casual clothes—or you always go to the supermarket in jeans and a T-shirt—you're reinforcing the tendency to be embarrassed when you get dressed up. If you make a habit of looking a little better in your off-duty hours—a little better for the supermarket—people won't be so surprised to see you looking good. And you won't feel so out of character when you do dress up.

Indeed, home is the best place to experiment with looking better because it's the least risky. The more you get the hang of it, the easier it will be to take the next steps at work and in your social life.

For example, learn to walk in high heels at home. That doesn't mean you should live in them, only that when you get used to doing the things you have to do or want to do dressed a little better than before, you'll become more and more comfortable looking *good*—not just passable. And when you feel comfortable looking good, you'll start to feel confident looking *terrific*.

Dressing for Your Social Life

As a Sporty-Casual, you may have mixed feelings about your social life. You really enjoy people, but that being so, you wonder why you don't enjoy yourself more when you have a chance to be with them and the occasion is special. Could it be that you'd like to be a little more special yourself, but you're uncomfortable when you have to be all dressed up?

Have you even caught yourself hoping you wouldn't be invited somewhere because you just can't face a whole evening of feeling stiff and unnatural in the clothes you think you have to wear? Don't ever turn down an invitation for *that* reason again.

Since dressing up causes you so much anxiety, you put off thinking about it (as most of us do). When you have to get it all together at the last minute—hair, makeup, clothes—*it doesn't work.* Because you don't have the right pieces, the right accoutrements. Since it's unrehearsed, it'll never feel like you. None of that means you have to give up. It really isn't as hard as it may seem to get the results you want.

You don't have to change everything overnight. Take it in stages. Don't go glamorous all of a sudden. You won't feel natural—and you won't look natural. Edge into a dressier look with a pretty blouse, slimmer, higher heels (but only those you can comfortably walk in). If you don't feel good wearing a soft dress, wear pants. Even pants can be dressy—and feminine, too. (Think of Mary Tyler Moore and Stefanie Powers.)

There's a way to feel natural even when you're looking special. Just turn the page to see sporty-casual clothes for a total life-style.

Dressing for Your Job

Administrative Level

Basic

Can you ever achieve the professional look in a sweater and skirt? This is the outfit that proves you can. The special touch that pulls it off? A double-breasted sweater for a more formal third layer. Sporty's basic security—a comfortable sweater, a plaid skirt—is here, yet the overall effect is one of easygoing professionalism.

Dressing for Your Job

Administrative Level

Creative

This is sweater-and-skirt dressing with a difference—actually, a number of differences. New proportions for the sweater and skirt, for one; no blouse under the sweater; and the sweater belted instead of loose. Further stretching of the rules: unconventional coordinates, a *little* more show of skin. The end result? Office attire that's appropriate, but still casual.

Dressing for Your Job

Managerial Level

Basic

Separates so compatible they have the look of a suit. Little touches that make a difference—softening the look with the bow, formalizing it with a belt. In this, Sporty can still feel safe. She still has the uniform of a suit, but the overall effect is Sporty at her best: coordinated, but informal.

Dressing for Your Job

Managerial Level

Creative

Unmatched, separates can still have a finished, professional look. The extra effort taken shows in a number of ways, such as putting separates together to achieve a coordinated look . . . an easier attitude. For Sporty, the exhilarating risk is that she's not "all buttoned up" in the conventional way. The result? Fashion adapted to her own standards of comfort.

*Basic**

This is Sporty's favorite version of a suit:
unmatched pieces. Unmatched but not un-
coordinated. The solid-color sweater-vest
coordinated with a color in the tweed. And
there's the jaunty fashion touch of belt
and gloves. For Sporty, the basic security
is clear—a comfortable blazer, a traditional crisp-collared shirt—but the overall
effect is an authoritative statement even
though the outfit is a suit that's not a suit.

*On the Executive Level a suit is always Basic
and universally respected in the working world.
(It's no longer seen as an attempt to imitate men.)
Your personal choice of suit shape and how you
accessorize it are what make it individual and
right for your image-type.

Dressing for Your Home Life

Weeknights After Work

*Creative**

It's a jumpsuit—casual, comfortable, relaxed, and the very essence of Sporty. Even so, attention has been paid, extra effort evident, in the right belt, socks, and shoes. In choosing a jumpsuit at all, Sporty has been venturesome because it's a fashion statement. And it pays off handsomely in the overall effect: an outfit that's so comfortable, yet so current.

*At home, the jumpsuit is the one category that pushes against the parameters of each image-type in exactly the way each type needs it the most. For Sporty, Classic, and Feminine a jumpsuit is Creative; for Exotic, Arty, and Sexy, it's Basic.

Dressing for Your Home Life

Weekend Dressing

Basic

This is classic Sporty—with a twist of fun in top-to-bottom Argyles. And it doesn't stop there. Notice her chic accessory of a twisted neck-scarf, and the pushed-up sleeves. Notice, too, the basic security is all there in the Argyles (easy cardigan, knee socks) and the flat shoes. The end result? A pulled together look in true Sporty-Casual tradition.

Dressing for Your Home Life

Weekend Dressing

Creative

This is "thrown-together" fashion that is very much on purpose, and with knowing skill. The extra effort is evident in the layering of separates—and so is the willingness to take a risk: the bolero sweater and cropped pants, adding up to a clear fashion statement. The overall effect? Real, down-to-earth clothes fashioned for an active life.

Dressing for Your Social Life

Cocktail Party

Basic

The tuxedo effect—simple, stylized—is, psychologically, Sporty's most comfortable way to go formal. Ruffles give it a feminine touch . . . the pussycat bow makes a bold statement. Yet it's a tailored shirt and pants—Sporty's basic security. The overall effect? An acceptable uniform—with dash.

Dressing for Your Social Life

Cocktail Party

Creative

This is the glamorized suit at its most wearable. Tailored, yes, but with a "look-at-me" camisole that shows Sporty made an extra effort. The attention-getting glitter and the low-cut exposure say she's dared to take a chance. The payoff? A suit for Sporty that's *exciting*!

Dressing for Your Social Life

Casual Evenings at a Friend's

Basic

For Sporty, this is casual dress-up at its most natural: a finished look of easy informality. Belting the sweater in for form and wearing balletlike slippers (instead of the usual loafers) are the special touches, yet the basic security that matters so much to Sporty is still there in the comfort and familiarity of a turtleneck and pants. The overall effect? Pants made special enough to go out to dinner.

Dressing for Your Social Life

Casual Evenings at a Friend's

Creative

This look still says Sporty, but it's Sporty reaching for fashion. The extra effort shows in the new silhouette: casual, yet timelessly current. The risk she's dared to take here—and it's so unexpected—is the total absence of Prep. The overall effect? Smashing—and still unmistakably Sporty.

Dressing for Your Social Life

Dinner at a Fine Restaurant

Sporty dresses for herself (casual) and for the occasion (dressy)—and feels good about both. This top feels the same as her daytime shirt, but for her, the shine of satin stripes says it's evening. So does the relaxed, open neckline and the appropriate accessories of earrings and loose necklace. There's nothing to make her feel stiff and pretentious, everything to make her feel dressed up yet still free. The overall effect? Easy glamour and, most important for Sporty-Casual, relaxed comfort.

These examples of Basic and Creative dressing for the Sporty-Casual have been deliberately chosen to point up the contrast as sharply as possible in order to make it clear how wide a choice is open to you—*within the parameters of your type.* The pieces of the minimal wardrobe that follow fall somewhere in the middle. By definition, a minimal wardrobe has to give you the most useful and basic pieces you need to start with. Once you have these, once your "center" is covered, you're free to extend your wardrobe with as many of the more purely Basic or Creative elements as you want, so long as they are *within your type.*

Minimal Wardrobe for the Sporty-Casual

1. Camel-and-navy herringbone blazer

2. Navy double-breasted sweater jacket

3. Heavy red silk patch-pocket shirt

4. Navy cotton blouse; white-and-red foulard tie

5. White popcorn sweater

6. Navy flannel pleated skirt

7. Camel hair dirndl skirt

8. Camel hair pleated pants

9. Beige silk dress with red stripes

10. Natural woven leather belt

11. Navy lizard belt

12. Natural leather shoulder bag

13. Navy leather medium-heeled pumps

14. Gold twist stud earrings

15. Gold link chain

Colors and Textures for the Sporty-Casual

As a Sporty-Casual, you're most at ease in modified Preppy colors and pure fabrics. For a business luncheon, you can choose a simple gray flannel suit with a white blouse of textured linen. Daytimes are no problem for you; khaki, clear red, gray flannel, brown tweed, lots of navy, beiges, denim blue, and pink as an accent color are likely to be your favorites—and they're all appropriate.

Evenings are your worry. You're not comfortable in dressy clothes, so you're likely to wear the soft pastels you've been wedded to since childhood. Why not try ivory instead? Or black. With the proper use of color you can carry the casual separates look you love even into evening—for example, try a buff suede skirt with a dressy cream cashmere sweater. Try to wean yourself away from the practical colors you're so strongly drawn to. You don't always have to put "safety first." As it is, even when you do wear primary colors—in the summer, say—you're too timid about how to combine them, what to wear with them. Feel at ease in the core colors of the soft neutrals listed here—then go for a little excitement in the accent colors and textures.

Core Colors

Beige
Camel
Gray
Brown
Navy

Accent Colors

White
Pink
Yellow
Green
Blue
Red

Textures

Cotton
Cable knit
Popcorn knit
Denim
Canvas
Seersucker
Polyester or wool gabardine
Fine-wale corduroy
Camel hair
Wool flannel
Wool tweed
Silk
Taffeta
Velveteen

Accessories as Your Trademark

Your most fundamental mistake is to settle for jewelry that's too small and insignificant. You might push yourself to wear jewelry of medium scale—especially now since "bold and large" is in. On you, bold and large would be wrong because it would be too strong for your natural look. So for you, bold should be medium-scale earrings instead of tiny studs, a medium-weight chain instead of baby-fine links. Your next goal should be to step up the variety of your accessories and change them more often with each outfit. You might try ivory earrings in the summer, a more dramatic belt buckle, a red clutch bag.

Your outfits depend on finishing the look with small details—balancing the shine of gold earrings with a gold belt buckle, or a bracelet, or a gold lapel stickpin. If you make a point of "finishing" your outfit with that third layer of accessories, you'll achieve a look that's pulled-together and well-groomed. If you don't make the effort, your outfits will look too plain and unpolished because they'll be so simple, conservative, and probably of solid colors.

How to start? Your basic pieces—those that get worn with everything—should at least be of good quality. They don't have to cost a lot, but they should not be cheap-looking since they're all you wear, and you wear them all the time. Make it your goal to acquire six major accessories:

2 pairs of important gold or silver earrings bigger than you would be inclined to wear
1 striking gold or silver necklace
2 eye-catching belts (different shapes, different colors)
1 large pin for your jacket lapel (a crest or a stickpin)

Once you've amassed these, they'll give you such instant pizzazz, you'll be amazed at how proud you feel. And rightly so, because you'll have made the effort and it's paid off in a big way. Chances are you'll feel so "together," you won't need to spend any more money on clothes for a while. Over time, try to collect a range of accessories like these:

Sporty-Casual Accessories

Basic   **Creative**

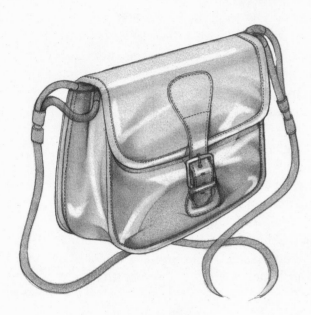

The Bag

Basic

Basic

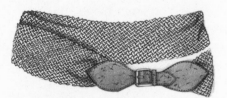

Creative

Creative

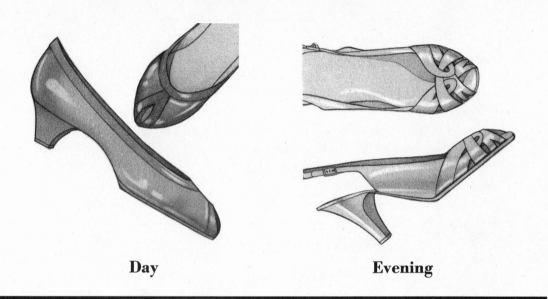

Day   **Evening**

Summary

Now that you've got an idea of what dressing to your image-type entails, now that you feel at home with the differences between Basic and Creative dressing, you're ready to explore the whole range of choices open to you. The boundaries of this range are what we call the parameters of your image-type—and what a wide area they cover!

Here are just a few of the ways you can vary your style of dressing and still be true to your type as a Sporty-Casual. You can play it Basic with your perennial favorite—a blazer jacket—or you can go Creative with just a blouse (but it must be an *important* blouse of elegant fabric, unusual neckline, or dramatic sleeves) and a belted skirt. You can create endless changes with tailored separates—skirt, blouse, and jacket or pants, shirt, and jacket—or break loose in a one-piece soft dress.

You may have a streak of wearing blouses and jackets with classic lapel collars and then again find you feel just as good, if not better, in blouses and jackets with shawl collars or no collars. You can show up in small stripes and plaids, then break out with a pattern in a medium-size floral. Some of the time you may prefer a stiff practical fabric like cotton, and when in a different mood, treat yourself to softer, more delicate fabrics like silk or knits. There may be days when only your low-heeled, practical walking shoes in brown or navy will do. And then there'll be times when your spirit insists on higher-heeled pumps in beige or red.

Week after week you may find yourself wearing your favorite 1-inch traditional leather belt in luggage brown. Suddenly you may want to be different with a 2½-inch-wide elastic cinch belt in red. Sometimes you'll feel your outfit needs minimal jewelry—small gold earrings and a classic belt—or no jewelry at all. And then again, you'll be wearing an outfit that cries for larger, bold earrings, choker necklace, and a belt with a stronger buckle *all at once.*

Even when it comes to makeup, you needn't feel hemmed in. One day only the "no-makeup" look may seem right, and the next, nothing but a finished face, with lipstick, blush, and a little mascara, will express your mood.

All this shows how important Basic and Creative dressing are for the Sporty-Casual. Basic is the quick way to help people recognize and understand you. It doesn't tell *all* about you, it just clues people into your general image-type, orients them to the territory. Once you telegraph your image-type, you can allow people to discover what makes you the unique individual you are. That's where Creative dressing comes in. Dressing creatively is to become constantly better at expressing your individuality. But only when you understand your true self can you begin to understand all the variety that true self affords you. You may find yourself expressing your individuality more directly, more subtly, more completely than ever before. Creative dressing is essentially a way of pushing against your image parameters. Of all the six image-types, the Sporty-Casual has the most to gain in doing just that *because it is the basic American image-type.* You start at dead center—with the clearest, cleanest, most natural canvas to work on—and you can take it in any direction you want.

More than half the women in America are Sporty-Casual—although most of them wish they were Classic or Exotic or Sexy. A good deal more than half the clothes offered in any season are designed for the Sporty-Casual, so you have the widest choice. Yes, you can stay in Basic. But even though Creative calls for more effort, it's so worthwhile. You, of all the image-types, stand to reap the highest reward for the effort you put in. Never forget, the aim is to project *your* best self, not somebody else's. Glamour for Sporty will not be the same as glamour for Sexy or Exotic.

And you should be glad that that's how it is. It makes for a much more interesting world—and it gives each of us a greater chance to make the most of our individuality.

The important thing to remember is that when I urge you to "push against your parameters," it's not for the sake of fashion, it's for *your* sake—the person you are and the person you want to become. When you care enough about yourself and about your world to let your clothes express *you*—not only the you people think they know, but the many sides of you that have barely surfaced yet—you'll feel yourself growing in ways you could hardly have imagined.

The more often you see yourself in an outfit that's right for you, the more your confidence will grow, and the more you'll realize other people's confidence in you is growing, too. When you dress in a way that fuses your image-type with the individual you are, you shine with a brightness and power people instantly sense and are attracted to.

3

If You're a
CLASSIC-ELEGANT

If you scored more B's than any other letter, you're the Classic-Elegant type along with:

Candice Bergen   *Jackie Onassis*
Lee Remick   *Catherine Deneuve*
Lauren Bacall   *Diane Sawyer*
Nancy Reagan   *Dina Merrill*

As a Classic-Elegant, you're in a group that includes some of the most admired women of our day, and the secret of your success can be summed up in one word: control. The reason you do so much—and do it so well—is that you have everything under control—your time, your work, your social life, your surroundings. That's because you think about what you want to do, analyze what you have to do to accomplish it, and then draw on the discipline you have to make it happen.

Though you do it all with quiet charm, some people are intimidated by your competence. You're highly organized: the one in the group who usually does the directing, instead of the detail work.

You don't waste time, not only because you're so well organized, but because you've thought things out so well in advance—boned up on the facts, learned about the people, figured out the timetable—that once you've set the course, everything proceeds to the goal without a hitch. You always try to do the right thing in any given situation, and usually succeed.

You look so calm, people find it hard to imagine you ever worry about anything. But you do, and what you're really communicating is caution. People see you as discerning; whatever you're trying to do you're intent on getting it right. And they think you succeed very well since everything about you always seems to be appropriate to the occasion—the way you dress, the way you talk, the way you relate to people.

Wherever you live—be it city or suburb, apartment or house—your restrained taste is apparent. Nothing gaudy or flashy or extreme would be part of your surroundings or part of your person.

Others see you, and admire you—and sometimes envy you—as having everything together, a seemingly effortless knack for organization of work and home life and appearance. You're respected for your good taste. You're liked because you're a good friend. And you're emulated for your style. People feel you add both solidity and flair to an occasion. Yet the consistent quality and "pulled-togetherness" of your style sometimes intimidates other women.

You're as careful about makeup and beauty routines as you are about everything else. Your eye makeup always goes with your outfit. Your hair, always immaculately clean and glossy, is in a neatly shaped, medium-length style, never curly or fussy. You're not particularly eager for change. Once you find your look, you keep it.

You want your clothes to whisper, not shout. For daytime, you prefer your clothes tailored, but feminine. For you, evening is very much an expensive black dress, but you always make sure you know what you're supposed to wear to an event by checking with the hostess. You're always dressed appropriately anyway because your taste is always understated and respectable in everyone's eyes.

You're perfectly willing to spend a lot of money on shoes and bags. Whenever they start to look the least bit shabby, you're quick to replace them. You'd rather buy an Yves St. Laurent silk blouse on sale than a copy for less money. If you can afford it, you'll buy top designer clothes, but you'll steer clear of those that are too identifiable. You don't experiment much. You find your hem-length and stick to it.

If you have clothing hangups, they're the extremes of your virtues. There's such a thing as looking *too* classic, for instance. You may be afraid to look sexy (even though you can, and perhaps at times *should*), afraid, in fact, of any real change. In a word, your biggest clothing handicap may simply be that you don't experiment enough or have fun with change.

A look through your closet will provide ample proof.

Colors and Combinations	Lots of black and cream (because it's chic, and so easy to mix and match)
	Also taupe, browns, and grays
	Colors mostly dusty shades—olive, burgundy, mauve; once in a while, a clear bright for accent
Fabrics	100 percent pure wool gabardine, wool challis, silk—not blends; nothing clinging or revealing
Textures	Smooth, non-bulky—only what tailors well; nothing too soft—that is, thin knits or sheers; nothing masculine—like the rougher tweeds
Patterns	Solids rather than prints (because they're more practical, easy to mix and match, "neater")
	If a print, probably not a floral, but a geometric (more orderly and subtle)
Accessories	Only those that say "This is the right thing"
	Understated, classic, but definitely status symbols: Tiffany gold chain, Gucci belt, Hermès scarf (or as close as you can get)

Your seasonal shopping patterns show the same natural talent for organization and time saving. You check the magazines, make lists of things to look for, do early buying by phone from fine-store fashion catalogs. You shop early (August/September for fall/winter, March/April for spring/summer). If you do spot-shopping, you go in for a specific thing—you won't get distracted by anything else. The only exception you allow yourself is when you come across something you really did intend to buy later. You've learned one of the basic secrets of good shopping: Buy it when you *see* it, not when you need it.

You understand the importance of seasonal updates, so you buy accessories of the season—a new lapel pin, belt, or shawl. And you follow the trend in legwear and shoe design.

What it all adds up to is this: as a Classic-Elegant you have a number of pluses going for you. The Classic-Elegant look is probably the most admired, always consistent, always in good taste. The message it sends is that of a capable, confident, gracious person. But there *are* a few minuses. For many women, the Classic-Elegant look can be too proper to allow them to relax, to be natural and easy in their body language. Classic elegance may also keep other women at a distance because its textures and colors are not warm and inviting, and your clothes are likely to be of a better quality than theirs. The look is chic and functional. The aim for you is to learn how to choose, and become comfortable with, clothes that make you a more approachable person, a woman of warmth and ease.

Clothes for the Classic-Elegant

Basic and Creative

Note: When you study the following illustrations, it's important to keep in mind that Basic means essentially "expected" for that type, and Creative means a looser, "less-expected" interpretation.

For the Classic-Elegant, the "expected" is solid gabardine skirts, tailored jackets, straight lines, excellent fit, quality fabrics, subtle colors, and a generally expensive look.

The looser, "less-expected" interpretation would consist of fluid skirts, softer jackets, less defined lines, easier fit, more textured fabrics, and a more relaxed look overall.

Dressing for Your Job

Of all the image-types, the Classic-Elegant is the most likely to be rewarded in the job market. You're the one who will probably have the fewest problems, because you know how to dress for the job. There are one or two things to watch out for, though. The higher your job level, the more important it is to show your professionalism with the expensive look of quality. This you know by instinct. However, make sure your clothes don't look *too* expensive. Sometimes your quality look can exceed your job. If your boss is a woman, it's important not to appear to be trying to outshine her. Men, particularly men of your level, are probably not "distanced" in the same way; the Classic-Elegant look is similar to their own code of dress and they respect it. Men understand quality of fabric, the subtlety of neutral colors, the look of fine tailoring—all of which are the expected attributes of their own clothes. However, unless you're at the top, don't let yourself look too formidable. Perfection tends to scare people, and you may do better on the job if you don't intimidate your co-workers.

Dressing for Your Home Life

The most important development for you in at-home attire is one-piece dressing—that is, jumpsuits. Since the casual occasion is a hurdle for you, the advent of the jumpsuit is a boon. You can slip into one and forget it. A jumpsuit works for you because it's not too "proper." It's neat, yet very relaxed. (You can put on an elegant belt and feel you're sending the right message.) When you wear a jumpsuit you're not putting people off in your own home.

At-home dressing for you was once a caftan. It was probably brocaded silk, straight down to the floor, and you had to be more careful in it than in your office clothes. The jumpsuit is your ticket to freedom. Until now, the closest you've been able to come is a silk shirt and a pair of slacks. You're on the right track. The line is right, but it's the choice of fabric that's forbidding. The same kind of outfit would work better, look less formal, and friendlier, in cotton or linen than in wool gabardine or silk. You're so accustomed to formal dressing you're not in tune with the relaxed dressing of today. While Sporty-Casual needs to practice feeling natural while looking formal, you, as a Classic-Elegant, need to practice feeling natural while looking relaxed.

You need to choose easy-care clothes you can forget about with a looser silhouette for your home life. Not only will they help you feel relaxed, they'll help other people relax around you. In very important ways, clothing dictates how you behave, how you move, what kind of time you have. Indeed, how you dress will determine whether people will interact with you. Classic-Elegant types need to be more approachable for their casual life.

Dressing for Your Social Life

Your drive for perfection never takes a day off. You're so concerned about your guests that you often don't sit at your own parties. You worry about the dinner menu, the table decor, the seating arrangements. If you're invited to a casual dinner at a friend's house, you're concerned about taking the right gift. You care too much to have a good time.

You're one of those rare people who actually feel uncomfortable when they're *supposed* to relax. Most people see you wearing "too good" clothes—pale gabardine pants and a matching silk shirt—even to a ball game or a family outing—and that makes *them* uncomfortable. Don't scare people away with your perfectionism. Learn to bend a little, modify your look for each occasion, and that means in silhouette as well as in fabric. You can still be classic and elegant, but in a relaxed way. Just turn the page to see classic-elegant clothes for a total life-style.

Dressing for Your Job

Administrative Level

Basic

One of Classic's favorite looks: softened suit-dressing, here embellished with the special touches of a fitted sweater and a finishing bow to underline the softness. The basic security that makes her happy? The look of a suit. The overall effect? Casually formal, exactly the note she wants to strike.

Dressing for Your Job

Administrative Level

Creative

In place of the usual suit, unusual layering. The extra effort shows in what *isn't* there. For once, she's not depending on a jacket. For her, the risk is actually wearing pants to work! The overall effect? Casual confidence, classic *and* elegant.

Dressing for Your Job

Managerial Level

Basic

Proper ensemble dressing, a favorite with Classic-Elegants everywhere, in business or not. The special touches that mark it up-to-the-minute are the longer layered lengths for chic. And for Classic, nothing beats the basic security of matched coordinates. The overriding effect? All business—and so very right.

Dressing for Your Job

Managerial Level

Creative

In contrast to ensemble dressing is the look of easy separates. Classic's willingness to make the extra effort, to take a chance, shows in the informality of a relaxed look and in the fashion twist of knotting a jacket. Yet here she goes even further: she dares to be seen in wrinkleable linen! And it's all worth it for the overall effect: casual confidence. A breakthrough for Classic-Elegant.

Dressing for Your Job

Executive Level

*Basic**

Tailored elegance is the look here—and nobody does it better than the Classic-Elegant. Her special touches add so much—the finest-quality fabric of flat wool gabardine, the sophistication of the dropped waist, the day-to-evening camisole blouse. The basic security this outfit offers is obvious: It's a timeless classic appropriate to any business situation. The overall effect? Authority with softness that goes smoothly from day into evening.

*On the Executive Level a suit is always Basic and universally respected in the working world. (It's no longer seen as an attempt to imitate men.) Your personal choice of suit shape and how you accessorize it are what make it individual and right for your image-type.

Dressing for Your Home Life

Weeknights After Work

*Creative**

Here is proof that formality is possible even in a jumpsuit. Still, the very fact that it *is* a jumpsuit shows that Classic is relaxed, and she should be given credit for that extra effort. Although this is a gamble for Classic, it has its rewards because she seems to be more at ease. The overall effect? An after work look elegant enough to meet even her standards.

*At home, the jumpsuit is the one category that pushes against the parameters of each image-type in exactly the way each type needs it the most. For Sporty, Classic, and Feminine a jumpsuit is Creative; for Exotic, Arty, and Sexy, it's Basic.

Dressing for Your Home Life

Weekend Dressing

Basic

The classic pantsuit at its purest, but with Classic's special touches: an unconstructed jacket with big pockets; fuller pants with pleats; and a monochromatic color scheme. The end result is a pantsuit of easier silhouette, but with the formality Classic relies on for her basic security.

Dressing for Your Home Life

Weekend Dressing

Creative

This is Classic in the newest version of a pants ensemble. The extra care and effort she's taken show up in all sorts of details: the longer softer jacket with dropped padded shoulders; the low-cut textured tank sweater; the softer, wider belt; the push-up sleeves; the strippy sandals. And, oh, the risks she's dared—not a single Basic touch. Softness and wrinkles she would never have permitted herself before. And more body exposure! The bottom line: very current coordination.

Dressing for Your Social Life

Cocktail Party

Basic

The heart of this look: the tuxedo coatdress with pearls to soften and the special touch of a satin collar. The basic security is plain to see in the simple man-tailoring and quality fabric. The overall effect? Glamorized authority, the evening extension of her office clothing.

Dressing for Your Social Life

Cocktail Party

Creative

A different look altogether: simple Grecian draping. As a result, no hard lines—and for Classic that's proof of extra effort. The risk she's taking is also clear: The bareness and softness mean real vulnerability. The end result? Classic-Elegant for once less austere, more feminine.

Dressing for Your Social Life

Casual Evenings at a Friend's

Basic

Classic's traditional favorite is the silk dress, and here the important shoulder line and the asymmetric bow are the special touches that make it distinctive. The basic security it offers is clear: this is what Classic considers her proper evening uniform. The overall effect? Approachable Classic-Elegant—standard, but always acceptable.

Dressing for Your Social Life

Casual Evenings at a Friend's

Creative

The look defined—an evening version of daytime separates; however, extra effort has been taken. She's put together a non-traditional combination of lightweight silk pajama pants with a heavier knit top. Yes, she's taken a calculated risk—pants for evening are not the usual for Classic—but the end result is worth it: a deliberate *fashion expression* that's unusually approachable for Classic-Elegant.

Dressing for Your Social Life

Dinner at a Fine Restaurant

This is Classic's signature look—understated elegance, through and through. The subtle sheen and the rich color of the charmeuse fabric make this her statement of evening glamour. The attention-catching focus is a quilted bib with a moving tassel that takes the place of a necklace. The end result? Elegant, quiet drama as only Classic could do it.

These examples of Basic and Creative dressing for the Classic-Elegant have been deliberately chosen to point up the contrast as sharply as possible in order to make it clear how wide a choice is open to you—*within the parameters of your type.* The pieces of the minimal wardrobe that follow fall somewhere in the middle. By definition, a minimal wardrobe has to give you the most useful and basic pieces you need to start with. Once you have these, once your "center" is covered, you're free to extend your wardrobe with as many of the more purely Basic and Creative elements as you want, so long as they are *within your type.*

Minimal Wardrobe for the Classic-Elegant

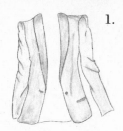

1.

Gray flannel easy jacket

2.

Taupe double-breasted
gabardine jacket

3.

Burgundy crepe blouse

4.

Gray tissue linen blouse

5.

Cream silk blouse

8.

Cream gabardine
pleated pants

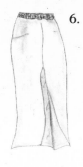

6.

Gray flannel
inverted pleated skirt

7.

Taupe gabardine
wrap skirt

9.

Gray-and-cream
silk dress

10.

Burgundy lizard belt

13.

Taupe lizard pump

11.

Taupe lizard bag

12.

Evening bag

15.

Gold earrings

14.

Burgundy suede pump

Colors and Textures for the Classic-Elegant

As a Classic-Elegant, you're never wishy-washy about anything—especially color. You wear either true, pure colors—navy, reds, blacks—or sophisticated "off" colors—teal or burgundy. If you wear a pastel, it will lean toward the neutral—cream or pale gray. If you're a strong personality (and most of the time you are), the stronger end of your spectrum will prevail, sometimes as an exciting contrast to basic cream.

For example, if you have an important business luncheon, or if you're speaking in front of a group, you might choose a simple cream gabardine suit with elegant tailoring, set off with a red silk blouse—a strikingly clear and dominant message.

For a cocktail party, your perennial favorites—black and cream—or the sophisticated "offs"—taupe and greige—are exactly right. They're an expression of your constant quest for quality and order in your life. If you're at all unsure about color, you won't go wrong if you choose designer clothes, because they give you the judgment of a proven professional not only in line but in color as well.

Core Colors

Cream
Beige
Taupe
Gray
Brown
Navy
Burgundy
Black

Accent Colors

Teal
Forest green
Burgundy
Red

Textures

Linen
Silk
Cashmere
Raw silk
Cavalry twill
Wool gabardine
Lightweight flannel
Crepe
Chiffon
Satin
Velvet

Accessories as Your Trademark

If you made a dream list of the accessories you'd most like to have, it could well read like this: Cartier tank watch, Gucci belt, Fendi bag, Ferragamo shoes, Hermès scarf, and diamond stud earrings from Tiffany's. Any or all of these would provide you with a sense of supreme confidence because they're so appropriate, and so timeless. You simply can't go wrong with them. They're status symbols, of course, and since they're of the highest quality possible, that means one less worry for you. These accessories say "close-to-perfect" on almost anything you would wear. And you'll save until you can buy the items on the list.

That's perfectly sound up to a point; however, there *are* other things to consider. If you're so intent on being perfect, you may miss out on being individual, which would be a pity. The less experience you get in learning how to express your individuality, the harder it is to do, and the more uncertain you become. While it's true your accessories are of very good quality, they may be too small. You're so concerned about not being gaudy that you may sacrifice impact. Perhaps it's time you borrowed from the other image-types and became a little more daring and unpredictable. With your casual wear, try wearing no jewelry; with your evening clothes, go more colorful and glamorous. See how the following touches can soften the intimidating "perfection" you strive for each day.

1. A fresh-picked flower in your buttonhole
2. A piece of antique lace at your collar or peeping out of your breast pocket
3. An interesting paisley challis shawl tossed over your solid-color coat or fine-flannel blazer
4. A belt with an eye-riveting buckle as a focal point on a cardigan sweater, or on a not-too-thick jacket, to give a flirtatious peplum silhouette

Build an accessory wardrobe that includes essentials like these:

Classic-Elegant Accessories

The Bag

Basic   **Creative**

Basic

Basic

Creative

Creative

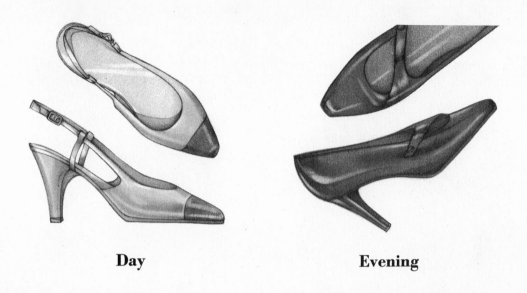

Day   **Evening**

Summary

Up to this point you've had a good sampling of just what Basic and Creative mean for your Classic-Elegant type in the main areas of job, home, and social life. Yet all the foregoing is just that—only a sample of the possibilities open to you. Now you're ready to discover for yourself the exciting choices available in the richly varied domain of Classic-Elegant.

Here are just a few variations to get you started. If you feel most comfortable with the most conservative look, you'll always insist on a tailored third layer. When you're ready for a change, you can try other kinds of third layers—a sleeveless tunic, perhaps; an easy-open vest; a shawl; or a ⅞ coat. Don't be surprised if you decide a blouse and skirt (the *right* blouse and skirt) or a dress alone, just finished with important accessories, is enough.

There'll be times when only a smooth wool gabardine jacket, collar down, sleeves down, will do. And just as surely there'll be a day when only a wrinkleable linen jacket (unlined), collar up, sleeves pushed up, seems right.

After weeks of wearing your favorite skirt type—slender, below-the-knee length—you may have an unaccountable yen for a full midi-skirt.

Just when your friends begin to think they never see you in anything but solid-color fabrics—cream silk or black cashmere—you'll break loose in a print, a taupe and burgundy floral challis for example.

Your "uniform" for weekends may be pleated gabardine slacks until the weekend you surprise everybody (including yourself) with cropped soft cotton pants.

If your signature shoe has always been a medium-heeled pump you may be amazed at how gloriously right you feel in an open sandal, flat or high-heeled.

You can go on serenely wearing sheer hose in bone, but be prepared for the little thrill of excitement when you switch to sheer, subtly textured hose that match the tone of your footwear—gray, off-black, sheer burgundy, sheer green.

If one day you realize your outfits are always one texture, you can discover how truly Classic-Elegant you can still be in a contrast of textures—bulky-knit sweater, tweed skirt, silk blouse.

If you wouldn't think of wearing anything but your usual three pieces of real jewelry—gold earrings, gold necklace, gold watch—think again. Think costume jewelry that changes with the needs of your outfits. You can mix the real with the fake. Wear different combinations—bigger earrings with no necklace; a choker collar with no earrings—and still be every inch the Classic-Elegant.

If you're used to finishing each outfit with a simple belt at the waist, discover the new elegance of a hip belt. Or even more so, the easier silhouette of a dress with no waist definition at all.

If you've always worn Classic-Elegant's traditional shoulder-length hairstyle, see what happens if you pull back one side with a comb for evening.

And though you probably match your eye makeup to your outfit, it may be even more of an eye-opener if you contrast it to your outfit—say, pink eye shadow when you're all in gray. If you're always well-made-up, even in your casual life, you might want to try an un-made-up look (makeup that looks so natural it's as if you aren't wearing any).

As a Classic-Elegant you may well be the envy of your friends. Many of them probably feel your image-type is the "perfect" one. Only you know that being perfect isn't all it's cracked up to be. Maybe you wish you could trade some of that perfection for a touch of the ease and naturalness characteristic of Sporty-Casual, or the frank womanliness of Sexy, or the independent individualism of Exotic.

Those are exactly the reasons why you must push against your parameters. There's more to Classic-Elegant than perfection. There's the need for growth and experimentation, the need to touch and be touched by other people, the need to let other sides of yourself see the light of day.

When you push yourself to explore all the territory between your image parameters, you can feel yourself growing as your horizons expand. You'll begin to see that it isn't perfection you're really aiming for. Rather, it's not to miss anything that is your rightful due. It's expressing your true self in all its human variety.

A good place to start is with the clothes you choose. Not just those at the Basic end of the spectrum (though you can't go wrong in those), but more and more, those that are at the Creative end, the ones that push against the borders of Classic-Elegant territory. The more comfortable you begin to feel in those, the more your world grows and the more fully alive you feel in it. When you can express all the things you feel you are, you won't feel so limited by having to be perfect.

4

If You're an
EXOTIC-DRAMATIC

If you scored more C's than any other letter, you're an Exotic-Dramatic,
one of a group that includes:

Bianca Jagger	Cher
Diana Ross	Mary McFadden
Diane Von Furstenberg	Marisa Berenson
Paloma Picasso	Grace Jones

As an Exotic-Dramatic, the thing you care most about is being one-of-a-kind. Unique. Original. A standout no matter what you're doing or where you are. Like the Arty-Offbeat, you don't seem to care what the world thinks about you, but unlike most Arty-Offbeats, you want the world to notice. And the world usually does—for many reasons.

First, you appear so confident and self-assured. You always seem to know the answers. The very way you carry yourself says you feel you're special. You can be very soft-spoken or highly flamboyant. Either way, you're always noticed.

You refuse to look like everybody else, so you go to great pains to make sure you don't. You're always ahead of the game in fashion, and dress with great flair. There's a certain stark, stylized quality about you in line, in color, in your very presence.

Wherever you live, it's not likely to be the average house or the average apartment. You feel most at home at the extremes: the *clean* look—all white, above, below, and around you—with minimal furnishings; or so much clutter you've raised it to an art form. You love using odd things for different purposes—old belt buckles as hair ornaments, antique bracelets for napkin rings, picture frames for mirrors. From time to time you'll turn the whole room around, just to make it different. You have a low tolerance for sameness, dullness, uniformity.

Your friends think you're impossible to buy a gift for. Your taste is so defined in your own mind, they can't second-guess you. And they just can't compete with your special flair.

In your approach to health and beauty, you'll try all sorts of new techniques in private, but you won't show off the results in public until they are perfected. Your lips may be shocking pink one day, raisin brown the next. Far from trying to camouflage an imperfection of face or body, you'll capitalize on it. You'll make it a signature that's yours alone.

When it comes to clothes, you won't let yourself look like anyone else. Style is your overriding concern. You'll study others, mull over trends and fads, but once you've decided on something, you make it your own. It becomes your personal stamp. You're not trendy or faddy, but if a style is right for you—padded shoulders, for instance—you'll keep it long after it's gone out of fashion. You like to collect unusual accessories—old shawls, one-of-a-kind belt buckles, antique chokers. Your aim is always to stand out in a crowd, to be striking. In pursuit of that aim, you'll be rather extravagant at times. You'll search far and wide, and spend a lot to maintain your clearly defined image.

Because you project such an aura of drama, people tend to see you as somewhat larger than life. You're admired for your style and presence, and you're emulated for your effect.

The clothes behind your closet door would probably run to something like this:

Colors and Combinations	Magenta and black, the heavy favorites
	Also whatever is strong, rich, deep: eggplant, teal, fuchsia
Patterns	Bold, dramatic florals; strong geometrics (no tiny checks or weak stripes)

Textures	Sophisticated combinations—for example, organza with a man's pinstripe wool
Accessories	Rule-breakers all, individually and together: tiny gold-knot earrings with a big chunk necklace; copper, gold, and bronze to mix at will; real mixed with fake

Your shopping patterns don't go according to the season. You shop all the time, you always have an eye out for the unusual accessory, the "perfect" objet d'art whenever and wherever you see it. Since any piece you find is so carefully chosen, it will serve as your signature for years— as long as you love it, as long as you want it to. If a skirt shape is perfect, you'll buy it when you see it because it's perfect for *you,* not simply because it's new and in fashion. You know your style so well, you can tell instantly whether any particular piece will fit into your image parameters. In fact, you probably know your parameters better than any other type.

Your special-event clothing needs are well-met by a superb black dress you can accessorize up or down. Its design is individual and right for almost any occasion, whether it's a gallery opening or opening night at the theater. Unlike Classic-Elegant's black dress, yours is probably asymmetric, or has an uneven hem, or an extreme, dramatic neckline.

Your main clothing hangups stem from your inability to compromise. For one thing, you don't have enough clothes for the simple reason you won't buy anything you don't think is perfect. At the same time, you don't have enough colors because you can't allow yourself to stray from the color you know looks best on you: black and more black. Good as it is on you, black needn't be—*shouldn't* be—your only color. For all the other colors that can look smashing on you, see page 69.

Your formula consists of a clothing background of simple, stylized lines with only a single strong accessory, such as a striking collar piece. In fact, your whole outfit may be planned around this special focal point. Before you even think about what clothes you're going to wear to a particular party, you're likely to decide which accessory you want to wear.

As an Exotic-Dramatic, how do you come out when it's all tallied up? You're sophisticated, independent, unique, savvy, and innovative— all important pluses. On the minus side, you can also come across as distant, intimidating, and difficult to please. These may be minuses, but they're not at all hard to change, especially with the right clothes.

Clothes for the Exotic-Dramatic

Basic and Creative

Note: When you analyze the outfits on the following pages it's important to keep in mind that Basic means essentially "expected" for that type; and Creative means a looser, "less-expected" interpretation.

For the Exotic-Dramatic, the "expected" is long, straight skirts, oversized jackets, stylized lines, exacting fit, extraordinary fabrics, unusual colors, and above all, the look of chic.

The looser, "less-expected" interpretation consists of softer skirts, ample sweater jackets, less-exaggerated lines, easier fit, simpler fabrics, and a generally more approachable look.

Dressing for Your Job

Your kind of dressing can blitz people anywhere, but especially at the office. In large part, your style is what's taken you as far as you've gone. It's a style that will always get you certain jobs, but it won't necessarily help you get ahead. Management may hesitate to promote you because you're so flamboyant. You stand out so much, you have to be terrific at your job to overcome their misgivings. They may think your talents are only clothes-deep.

You're putting yourself in the position of arousing expectations that are possibly beyond what you can produce. If you ease up on your style, tone down the drama from larger-than-life to life-size, other people's expectations of you may be reduced and they won't demand the impossible from you. Your co-workers won't think you're trying to one-up them. And you won't run the risk that your personality will be swamped by your clothes.

At the top you can do anything you want. You can set the tone for everybody else. You'll most likely always choose jobs that demand style, and you'll probably go furthest in a job that needs it—like being the editor of a top magazine. Take your cue from outfits like these for on-the-job dressing, which create drama with maximum impact.

Dressing for Your Job

Administrative Level

Basic

Bold, neat, organized—that's the triple combination that makes Exotic look right for business yet true-to-herself. The special touch here is restraint, keeping the accessories down to just complementary earrings. The basic security comes from the drama of a bold simple statement plus the fillip of the unexpected anklestrap shoe. The overall effect? A strong affirmation of capability.

Dressing for Your Job

Administrative Level

Creative

The look here is inexpensive layering, done with style. Extra effort shows in the unexpected use of an easy oversized third layer to finish the ensemble. For Exotic, the understated, unstructured ease is a risk well worth taking. The end result? Laid back, more approachable, nothing intimidating.

Dressing for Your Job

Managerial Level

Basic

This is how Exotic accomplishes the seemingly impossible: the use of menswear to look Exotic *and* businesslike at the same time. The special touches that bring it off are the softness of a contrasting neckscarf, the feminine accent of a wedge shoe. Her basic security is very much there in the drama of the oversized coat. The overall effect? Strength and confidence—in herself and in her job, surely one that demands style.

Dressing for Your Job

Managerial Level

Creative

The heart of this look is contrasting layers of knits. Exotic has made a special effort here, giving up the stark linear look, adding structure to softness with the leather belt, boots, and gloves. The calculated risk is plain: she's risking bulk for drama. The overall effect? A softer impact, but still strong.

Basic *

This soft, monochromatic layering has "executive" written all over it. But Exotic's special touches are very much in evidence: strong, simple jewelry; contrasting, wide hip belt; anklestrap high-heeled shoes; rolled-up sleeves. She's secure in the basics—the signature accessories, the high-fashion statement. The end result? A triumph of personal style, right for the occasion—a formal suit, out of layers of no-effort fashion.

*On the Executive Level a suit is always Basic and universally respected in the working world. (It's no longer seen as an attempt to imitate the male.) Your personal choice of suit shape and how you accessorize it are what make it individual and right for your image-type.

Dressing for Your Home Life

As an Exotic-Dramatic you're in your element at home because there you can be as exotic, as dramatic, as downright wild as you want. Any guest would know what you're like—and would come to be amazed, amused, shocked, and delighted—and never leave disappointed. One reason people enjoy being with you is that they like to stretch themselves, venture past their own boundaries, and you encourage them. Friends enjoy your passion for clothes and high drama, and they like to believe some of it rubs off on them. Clothes are almost a second career for you. You don't mind standing out like a beacon. You dress outrageously not to intimidate others, but to outdo yourself. It's like a private, continuing contest: can you top the drama you achieved last time?

For all that, you're not as self-confident as you ought to be. In a way, you set yourself up. Just as Sporty sets herself up to be embarrassed, and Classic sets herself up to be emulated, too often Exotic sets herself up to put herself down by setting an image so hard to maintain, she's not always sure she can bring it off.

Dressing for Your Social Life

Drama loves an audience, and you love every type of social occasion, from casual to formal, because you love looking your best. Your current Basic look is the same costumed look you've had all your life. Your drama is too staged. You hide in your style. People are often afraid to get to know you—you're so different, so formidable.

You've always known what your own best look is; you've always fabricated it. However, one small caution: it's one thing to stand out, it's quite another to overwhelm, especially on casual occasions. You can afford to ease up on the drama when the situation calls for it. Your goal is to be less self-conscious—and to make others less self-conscious around you. Break some of the rules, get outside the style. You'll always be exotic, even in shorts. Too often you use being exotic as a crutch. Concentrate on appropriateness first. Don't let it look as if your main reason for attending a dinner party was to show off your style. (But, at a cocktail party, it's dead right to be in full regalia. A big gathering is a great place to be exotic.)

On you, drama will take care of itself—as you'll see in the outfits that follow.

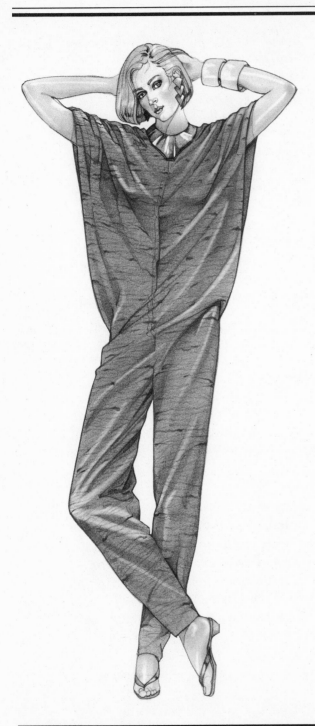

Dressing for Your Home Life

Weeknights After Work

*Basic**

This is one-piece dressing as only Exotic could bring it off. The calculated touch—omitting the signature belt; the exhilarating risk—taking a chance on total lack of structure. The overall effect? Exactly what she wants: ease with drama.

*At home, the jumpsuit is the one category that pushes against the parameters of each image-type in exactly the way each type needs it the most. For Sporty, Classic, and Feminine a jumpsuit is Creative; for Exotic, Arty, and Sexy, it's Basic.

Dressing for Your Home Life

Weekend Dressing

Basic

The heart of this look is layers of patterns and textures. The touches that make it special are: contrasting patterns; interesting bulk; dramatic belt covering the plain, ribbed bottom of the sweater; pants tucked into soft, crushy boots. Exotic's basic security here lies in the sophistication of mixed patterns and the focal-point belt. The overall effect is the usual bold statement, but this time it's a casual version with a somewhat quieter mix of patterns.

Dressing for Your Home Life

Weekend Dressing

Creative

This is the look of no hard edges, but the
extra effort put into it shows in many
ways: a shawl worn on one shoulder and
around the hips; the magenta of the shawl
on the charcoal gray of the jumpsuit; unmatched accessories—bronze collar,
chrome yellow bracelets. Add it all up and
it's a look that's softer than usual (and
that spells risk for Exotic). However, the
overall effect—approachability with no
lessening of drama—is well worth it.

Dressing for Your Social Life

Cocktail Party

Basic

For Exotic more than most, a cocktail party calls for high drama, and she does it as no one else could. She steps out in the most understated look in her repertoire, which is just the opposite of what anybody else would do and therefore the most attention-getting. The special touch here is the dramatic contrast of the taffeta bow tied to the side. Her basic security stems from the unadorned chic of the dress and the uniqueness of that bow. The overall effect? Exactly what she wants: stark simplicity plus impact.

Dressing for Your Social Life

Cocktail Party

Creative

The look here is that of an updated version of the flapper dress. The extra care she's taken to make it extra-special shows in the tiny finishing details of patterned stockings and patterned shoes, and in adding the head wrap to maintain the mood of the period. Never one to play it safe, Exotic takes the risk of omitting the expected big, bold jewelry. The end result? Softened glamour—a glitzy dress of sequins and bugle beads—in a softer-than-usual silhouette.

Dressing for Your Social Life

Casual Evenings at a Friend's

Basic

The look defined—a Cossack costume, out of a skirt and blouse. Note the special touches: a wide fashion belt to bring control to a big look; wearing the blouse as an overblouse; boots that follow the mood. Exotic's basic security—and familiar triumph—is turning the ordinary into a costume. The end result? What might be simply a skirt and blouse is turned into an ensemble thanks to Exotic's skill and caring.

Dressing for Your Social Life

Casual Evenings at a Friend's

Creative

This time it's pants and a blouse turned into a costume. The extra effort that brings it off is choosing only one important accessory, the belt—for impact, focus, and shaping. The worthwhile risk shows a body more exposed, its lines more defined. The overall effect? Again, the Cossack look, but soft, with big impact through simplicity.

Dressing for Your Social Life

Dinner at a Fine Restaurant

This is Exotic at her most assured and distinctive. A riveting print and the sophisticated line of a draped wrap take her to the outer limits of her image—and still she's in control. The wild hair, the big earrings, and the bareness of the plunging neckline balance the boldness of the print. A look that would overwhelm any other image-type simply underlines Exotic's own strength. The overall effect? A female powerhouse—enjoying it to the hilt.

These examples of Basic and Creative dressing for the Exotic-Dramatic have been deliberately chosen to point up the contrast as sharply as possible in order to make it clear how wide a choice is open to you—*within the parameters of your type.* The pieces of the minimal wardrobe that follow fall somewhere in the middle. By definition, a minimal wardrobe has to give you the most useful and basic pieces you need to start with. Once you have these, once your "center" is covered, you're free to extend your wardrobe with as many of the more purely Basic or Creative elements as you want, so long as they are *within your type.*

Minimal Wardrobe for the Exotic-Dramatic

1. Magenta faille one-button jacket

2. Black suede hip-band jacket

3. Bronze hammered satin blouse

4. Magenta suede top

5. White sweater with appliqués

8. Black leather pleated pants

9. Black and white shawl

6. Teal wool jersey skirt

7. Black suede wrap skirt

15. Black and cream necklace

12. Black lizard bag

13. Black lizard high-heeled pump

14. Bronze earrings

10. Black lizard belt

11. Teal suede wrap belt

Colors and Textures for the Exotic-Dramatic

Dominant colors for Exotic are sometimes the "pure" ones, sometimes the "off" ones. If you have to attend an important auction, you might wear an eggplant suit with a gold blouse. For a night at the theater, you'll wear black velvet harem pants with an emerald green silk top. In both instances, the contrast is striking. Your colors always have a hard edge—chrome yellow or deep purple. Even the off colors will have density—a bright teal or a sharp magenta. For you, color always has to be rich or vibrant.

Core Colors

White
Cream
Gold
Red
Royal blue
Purple
Eggplant
Black

Accent Colors

Pewter
Bronze
Turquoise
Teal
Magenta
Chartreuse
Chrome yellow
Emerald green

Textures

Linen
Silk jacquard
Hammered satin
Tissue suede
Raw silk
Wool jersey
Leather
Metallic knits
Gold lamé
Silk faille

Accessories as Your Trademark

Being an Exotic, you wear everything with such confidence and style, you don't follow the conventional rules in regard to accessories:

1. You never keep one theme in size and mood. You'll team small lapis stud earrings with a strong Byzantine cross necklace.
2. You mix accessories of different materials, for example brass with gold.
3. You'll mix the real with the fake. Plastic and ivory together are *right* on you.
4. You won't be concerned about balancing your accessories. You might choose to wear only huge earrings and nothing else. Sporty has to balance a bit of glitter from a gold belt buckle with medium-size gold earrings, and her red buttons with a red clutch bag. Exotic can get away with wearing a whole outfit of palest yellow, then stun your eye with a large royal blue shoulder bag!
5. You won't limit yourself to only one strong focal point. You'll wear a strong necklace with a strong bracelet.

You're so naturally drawn to the striking and unusual, be it pendant, pin, or belt, that you seldom need to worry whether you've made the right choice. You *may* need to think more about just how you wear your accessories—with what outfit and in what combinations—because it's so easy to wear the same piece the same way all the time. If you've chosen an African mask to wear on a heavy gold chain, try it next time as a belt buckle on a suede sash. Once you fall in love with a piece, you stay in love with it, which is all the more reason to keep it fresh by changing how you wear it.

Not all Exotics are five-foot-ten with long black hair. Some are five-foot-one with short dark hair. If you're one of those, you may have to be a little more creative than usual. Don't try to wear more than one large exotic accessory at a time. If you do, balance them carefully. Even if you're short, your statement of individuality can be just as strong as that of a taller Exotic. Though the accessories you choose may have to be scaled down, Exotic is always a strong image. And since you choose to wear accessories on a stark background, you're always dramatic.

One last point. However Exotic you may be, consider where you're going that day. It's one thing to wear your head wrapped to a farewell party on the *QE II,* it's quite another to wear it to a first meeting with the bank officer who's going to approve your loan. It's fine to proclaim that you're different, but it's also irritating to rattle five noisy bangle bracelets while on the job. It may be a stroke of genius to wear the perfect large-scale pin to finish the hip-line on your new evening dress, but it may show less than good sense if you run the risk of stabbing your partner with it.

As an Exotic, you always add drama to any occasion or group. If you can avoid the extremes that make people uncomfortable, you're sure of a warm welcome anywhere, because you heighten interest as soon as you appear. Build your accessory collection with choices like these:

Exotic-Dramatic Accessories

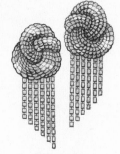

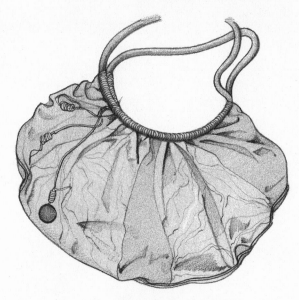

The Bag

Basic

Creative

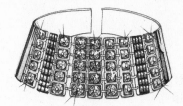

Basic

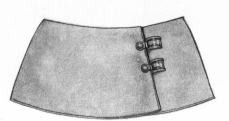

Basic

Creative

Creative

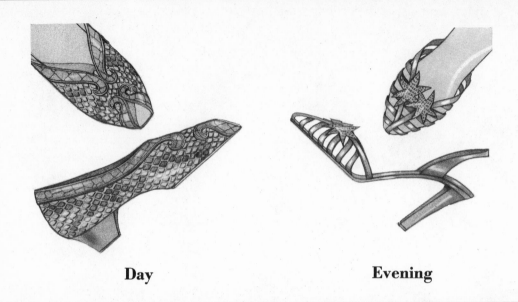

Day   **Evening**

Summary

For Exotic-Dramatic, a whole wonderful range of fashion choices exists between the parameters of your image-type, between what's Basic for you and what's Creative. You can roam at will throughout this terrain and still feel safe and confident that you'll always be true to yourself, because you'll be true to your type.

You can come on the scene in an outfit that's totally thought through for a calculated, structured, stylized look. Or show up in something with a loose casual air, less structured, but still stylized. You may decide you'll achieve your Exotic image by conforming to the current fashion. Or, in another mood on a different day, reach the same goal ignoring—or twisting—the latest fashion—say, showing up wearing a long skirt when everyone else is in short ones.

Sometimes you won't feel dressed without a strong signature piece as an accessory. And then again, you might feel your best in an outfit that stands by itself unadorned.

As an Exotic, you're the only image-type whose Basic dressing is so dramatic and out of the ordinary that for you Creative dressing is actually dressing more conservative in order to be more approachable. It's going against the anticipated for your image-type. People are so accustomed to impact and drama in your style that they read it into you even when you're wearing something very quiet, even mainstream.

This readiness to assume that whatever you do is bound to be right extends even to what you decide to do with your hair. You may decide your hair will be your signature and so you always wear it in the same sleek style. Yet if you change it to suit your mood, people will easily come to take the change as your signature, too.

Of all the image-types, you're the one most likely to limit yourself to only your few most flattering colors, the ones you think reflect your personality. But if you're really smitten by an outfit in a color that's not one of "yours," you're willing to go Creative and try it—and as a result, find yourself widening your range.

In the matter of necklines, you've always gone to extremes—they're either buttoned up high, or plunging low. But one day you'll discover the kick that comes from knowing just how many buttons to leave undone to make even the most ordinary collar look chic.

The jacket you're wearing today may be the same length and shape you discovered was "you" at fifteen. But that doesn't stop you from experimenting with new silhouettes, always hoping to top your original.

Your eye makeup is always strong and perfectly done, but for the casual times of your life, you're willing to soften it.

Exotic-Dramatic may well be the one who has the most fun with clothes. You have talent for finding the perfect one-of-a-kind accessory, an instinct for displaying it to best effect. Your understanding of the dramatic is so keen it's almost a sixth sense.

However, you may be so single-minded in your drive for impact that you don't give other sides of you a chance to come out and be recognized. That's why it may be as important for you to push against your parameters as it is for some of the other less image-oriented types.

As an Exotic, you will always command attention. What you may be missing out on is the chance to widen your scope, to encourage people to respond to the person you are—the core of you, not just your "packaging." Don't forget the fun of adding a bit of femininity, a dash of sexiness, or a touch of Sporty's casual comfort. You'll still be Exotic-Dramatic, but with a little twist of unpredictability.

5

If You're an

ARTY-OFFBEAT

If you scored more D's than any other letter, you're an Arty-Offbeat, right along with:

Barbra Streisand   *Diane Keaton*
Liza Minnelli   *Carly Simon*
Tina Turner   *Cyndi Lauper*
Madonna   *Goldie Hawn*

Since you're an Arty-Offbeat, the key phrase for you is "free-spirit." You're first, last, and always your own woman. Not that you march through life announcing it with brass bands. You just live it—sometimes so quietly that it takes a while before people realize how stubbornly individual you are.

You're a private person. You're on your own time clock, uncompetitive with other people and unrushed by the world. (You're often late, but you get there.) You may not have a lot of money, but it doesn't bother you. You don't feel you need riches. Your expenses are low because you're not a compulsive shopper. If you can, you'll pick up your clothes in a flea market or spot them in a thrift shop.

Wherever you live—be it a loft, a single room in a brownstone, a walk-up in the city, an old farmhouse, or a converted barn in the country—the place is a crazy-quilt of textures, crammed with the unique and the personal, the collected mementos of your life. There's very little that's new and shiny—but for you, everything has its own patina of love and memory.

When it comes to makeup you wear either none, or lots—depending on where you're going. Your eyes are your focal point, and you're constantly experimenting for more dramatic looks. You like dramatic hairstyles, too—long frizz or very short punk cuts are your favorites. You might have streaks, but more likely your hair is a strong natural color.

In regard to clothes, you abide by two main principles: they have to be individual, and they needn't cost a lot of money. You can't bear to look like anybody else, even in one outfit, even for one day. You must "own" the look, so you create it yourself. You never read fashion magazines or buy an outfit out of a store window. You have to put every combination together your own way with scarves as belts, earrings as pins, old pieces mixed with new. You love natural fibers and textures . . . love to make your own mix-and-match layers of clothes. You aim for interesting rather than chic combinations. As for spending a lot of money on clothes, you think that's downright sinful. You take pride in *not* spending it, not going to the store to lay out your dollars just to look like everyone else. It's not that you're stingy. You have an eye for your own style and once in a while, you splurge on something you love. You'd rather "do it yourself" and create your own one-of-a-kind look.

Individual as you feel your image to be, there are pitfalls to be avoided. If you always rebel in your dress and make it wildly unusual, you may begin to lose a presentable look, and you'll risk shutting yourself out of other circles. You'll find it harder to socialize with certain men and female friends who are sporty or feminine or elegant or exotic because the "unique" look you're so proud of creates a gap that may make both sides uncomfortable.

Your image does have certain pluses. For one thing, it doesn't have to cost a lot because your standard is not the standard of most other shoppers—not status or name or conventional taste or look. Your standard is whatever says "individuality" to you, and that can be anything, found anywhere. So you have the fun of always keeping your eyes open anywhere you may be, whether it's a foreign bazaar, an out-of-the-way thrift shop, an Army-Navy store, or your mother's attic. You "see" your fashion where others don't.

You have another great advantage. Nothing can be called "wrong." It's hard for even other Arty-Offbeats to criticize how you put yourself together. You're vulnerable only if you haven't put in any creative effort.

One look inside your closet would probably reveal the following:

Colors and Combinations	Mostly dark—with a few neon accents
	No pastels or medium colors
	Color combinations often unusual, offbeat—fuchsia and burgundy, curry and purple
Fabrics and Textures	Rough tweeds, nubby cottons, sculptured velveteens, antique lace; mixed textures
Patterns	From menswear pinstripes to antique brocades, florals to tweeds
	Daring mixtures of patterns—even large flowers with geometrics
Accessories	Large pouchy leather or suede bags, hammered silver and brass jewelry, 1940s necklaces, period pieces from delicate to strong

Like everything else about you, your shopping patterns are anything but rigid and routine. If you see something you like in a shop window, you'll buy it on the spot. You frequent auctions, secondhand stores, and craft fairs . . . and you're in bliss if you discover an old trunk of clothing from the twenties in an attic.

Your seasonal updates are usually confined to jewelry and outrageous belts. And interesting versions of legwear.

How to sum up the Arty-Offbeat? On the plus side: individual, unique, interesting, creative, *fun!* On the minus side: rebellious, foreign, unadaptable.

Your style of dressing is so individual, your outfits so one-of-a-kind, you have no worry about standing out in the crowd. Your clothes already set you apart. The problem is, it may be too far apart. They shouldn't isolate you. The right clothes can help you keep your individuality and still feel warmly welcomed into other worlds, other relationships—as you'll see in the following pages.

Clothes for the Arty-Offbeat

Basic and Creative

Note: When you study the illustrations in the following pages it's important to keep in mind that Basic means essentially "expected" for that type; and Creative means a looser, "less-expected" interpretation.

For Arty-Offbeat, the "expected" is mini- or long skirts, no jackets, loose tops, not much fit, interesting fabrics, murky colors, and a very relaxed look.

The looser, "less-expected" interpretation would be less exaggerated skirts, the third layer of a jacket, more controlled lines, closer fit, flatter fabrics, a generally presentable appearance.

Dressing for Your Job

You are not likely to wind up at a straight desk job. The natural order of things just doesn't let this happen. You'll probably find yourself in a job where your individuality is accepted. After all, if you didn't change for the interview, and they hired you, you've obviously got something they want and need.

On the other hand, important as it may be to remain true to yourself—even on the job—it's wise not to look too far out of the mainstream, especially in the more conventional jobs. You can still be you—and original—without looking like a stray from another culture, as these outfits prove.

Dressing for Your Job

Administrative Level

Basic

This is how that most conventional two-some—a blouse and skirt—can look uniquely Arty yet right for work. The shirt, bow tie, and belt from the men's department; the drawstring waistband of the skirt pulled tight in potato-sack fashion; and the Mary Jane shoes are all Arty's signature touches. For Arty, basic security always stems from an expression of her individuality—very much in evidence here in her glasses and bow tie. The end result is a small triumph: the simplest of separates with a unique signature of crisp authority.

Dressing for Your Job

Administrative Level

Creative

This is the look of today's jumper—the jumper made hip—and it didn't "just happen." It's the careful balance of accessories that brings it off, proof of the extra effort that went into it. The gamble for Arty? Arty's challenge to Preppy . . . Arty's little-girl vulnerability, there for all to see. The end result? A finished and controlled relaxedness.

Dressing for Your Job

Managerial Level

Basic

This is one of Arty's favorite looks: interesting layers of textures. The special touches—Exotic's shawl, Sporty's belt, Classic's shirt, Feminine's bow, and Arty's own 1940s sweater and boots—add up to a uniquely eclectic and individual mix to achieve perfect balance. As always, her basic security lies in expressing her individuality, but this time in a way indeed rare for her: She's studiedly coordinated. The overall effect? A total put-together with wonderful originality.

Dressing for Your Job

Managerial Level

Creative

One sleek rich layer, not usual for Arty, but made her own by her distinctive choice of accessories. The special touches: a low-slung belt, strong but easy, to give line to the dress; the striking scarf, as only Arty could do it, suede on suede; and the interesting balance of shorter boots and colored opaque hose. The overall effect? A conventional dress turned Arty because it's long and suede—and with her own special accessories, it's no longer conventional.

Dressing for Your Job

Executive Level

*Basic**

This is a look that brings off what some less imaginative souls would consider impossible: melding Arty's passion for costume with the cool realities of business. Period accessories of hat, blouse, shoes, and walking stick are the special touches that underline the old-world charm of the outfit. Arty can still have the basic security of being true to herself—even in the uniform of a suit, she is still breaking the mold to be individual. The overall effect? A unique statement of daringly creative authority.

*On the Executive Level a suit is always Basic and universally respected in the working world. (It's no longer seen as an attempt to imitate men.) Your personal choice of suit shape and how you accessorize it are what make it individual and right for your image-type.

Dressing for Your Home Life

Home is where you feel most like yourself—and most free. Free of conventional pressures to conform. So home can be the arena where you really shine in your personal style. But don't stray so far out that you find it difficult to go conventional when you have to.

Even though you, more than any other type, can get away with a far-out look, it's well worth your while to aim for a little more control. Practice small touches of the conventional by finishing your look with the right accessory or top layer, even at home. If you learn to feel comfortable with a finished look at home, it will be easier to take a finished look out into the world. You'll already own it. For Arty, there's nothing that says individual can't live with conventional.

Dressing for Your Social Life

You're so used to looking different from other people—because you take pride in it—you may forget to look different from yourself. Arty-Offbeat often wears the same type of clothes all the time without realizing it. Haven't you caught yourself thinking if you put on your dressy earrings and drape your glitter scarf around your neck you'll be fine as is for a cocktail party? You owe your audience more than that. Pay homage to the occasion. Surprise people with a more appropriate outfit. Show them you can change and be interesting in your own unique style.

It's quite possible to fit in, and still offer originality as well as variety—as you'll see by these examples.

Dressing for Your Home Life

Weeknights After Work

Basic *

This is Arty as Harem Gypsy—one of her favorite selves: offbeat, seductive. It's not a look that just "happened" even though it looks so relaxed and playful. For Arty, it took real discipline to keep it down to the simplicity of a one-piece jumpsuit. In fact, it took more than discipline, it called for real risk-taking—daring to define her body and pass up the usual layers of protection. The overall effect? Neat and defined (unusual for her) with a touch of personal clutter.

*At home, the jumpsuit is the one category that pushes against the parameters of each image-type in exactly the way each type needs it the most. For Sporty, Classic, and Feminine a jumpsuit is Creative; for Exotic, Arty, and Sexy, it's Basic.

Dressing for Your Home Life

Weekend Dressing

Basic

Top to toe, the look is Annie Hall, the prototype of Arty-Offbeat. Just count the special touches: the 1940s jacket, a man's loose necktie, the scarf used as a belt, baggy pants tapering at the ankles, men's oxfords. Offbeat as it all may be, the basic security is clear to see in the perfected techniques of sloppy layering, the comforting ties to another era. The overall effect? A new angle on the men's wear look: arty and fun.

Dressing for Your Home Life

Weekend Dressing

Creative

This is the esoteric Arty, stylized and simple. And the care it took is apparent in both plus (the fashion boot in purple) and minus (omitting the usual layers and jewelry). For Arty, besides real effort, there's real risk: facing the world in just one layer, and showing lots of leg. The end result is well worth it: Arty as sleek, clean, and unencumbered—totally unexpected.

Dressing for Your Social Life

Cocktail Party

Basic

This is Arty-Offbeat to the nth degree.
Each of the special touches is Arty in cap-
ital letters: the richly patterned shawl; the
oversized belt; the signature boots. But
for all that boldness, all that jazz, her
basic security is well looked after. She's
got murky colors and lots of fabric to hide
her body under. The overall effect? Intri-
cate armor to draw interest, yet at the
same time provide protection.

Dressing for Your Social Life

Cocktail Party

Creative

This is the very essence of Arty-Offbeat: simplified and rarefied—and they don't come easy. It takes real caring, real effort for a real Arty to pare down the usual layers and pieces to one long, lean sweater and a sinuous skirt. It also takes real daring to show off her body in a single layer of fabric that's both black and thin. The overall effect? A rare kind of vulnerability that's all but irresistible.

Dressing for Your Social Life

Casual Evenings at a Friend's

Basic

Arty's talent for striking originality is nowhere more clearly demonstrated than in what she can do with that standard twosome—a sweater and skirt. It's her special touch that makes all the difference: a dramatic one-of-a-kind sweater; the long, full skirt for balance; the wide cummerbund sash belt. Even what's *not* there—no layers of clothing, just layers of detail—adds to the impact. What Arty gloats over in her heart, though—the source of her secret security—is that she's standing out from the crowd, without overspending. The end result? Individuality of personal style in every element.

Dressing for Your Social Life

Casual Evenings at a Friend's

Creative

Here, Arty achieves the unexpected in a
jacket and skirt because she cares enough
to pass up the obvious. Instead of pairing
a safari jacket with jeans, she teams it
with the unusual: a skirt. It's a gamble,
it's creative—mixing conventional pieces
to achieve a distinctive, unconventional result—and it pays off. The overall effect is
a jacket and skirt that add up to pizzazz.

Dressing for Your Social Life

Dinner at a Fine Restaurant

The look here is a surprise mix of elements distilled into an intensely personal statement, unmistakably Arty: the hand-painted print reflects her love of craft; the looseness of her blouse, her need for comfort; her long porcelain earrings are sculpture to her; and the finishing touch of gold braid on her blouse is her tribute to glamour. The end result? A fierce loyalty to individuality shines in every detail, yet the total turnout exactly fits the requirements of the occasion.

The preceding examples of Basic and Creative dressing for the Arty-Offbeat have been deliberately chosen to point up the contrast as sharply as possible in order to make it clear how wide a breadth of choice is open to you—*within the parameters of your type.* The pieces of the minimal wardrobe that follow fall somewhere in the middle. By definition, a minimal wardrobe has to give you the most useful and basic pieces you need to start with. Once you have these, once your "center" is covered, you're free to extend your wardrobe with as many of the more purely Basic or Creative elements as you want, so long as they are *within your type.*

Minimal Wardrobe for the Arty-Offbeat

1. Khaki shirt jacket

2. Black cotton vest

3. Burgundy blouse

4. Curry gauze blouse

5. Khaki ribbon sweater

6. Burgundy-and-curry challis skirt

7. Khaki and black skirt

8. Eggplant burlap pants

9. Khaki jumpsuit

10. Challis shawl

11. Twisted leather belt

12. Black ballet slippers

13. Black leather boots

14. Earrings

15. Pewter necklace

Colors and Textures for the Arty-Offbeat

As an Arty, you love to play with color. It's a part of the fun you have with fashion. You'll use all the colors and mix them in outlandish ways that somehow seem to work. (You'll even put fuchsia and chartreuse together! (And you play with color wherever you go. For that gallery opening, for instance, your skirt might be a fuchsia mini—or a purple maxi—topped off with a teal suede cropped-top or an oversized man's shirt in a pinstripe. Either might be finished with a shawl you saw on someone's piano. In your ongoing rebellion against traditional combinations, you count on color and texture to keep you free.

Core Colors

Khaki
Olive
Rust
Bottle green
Eggplant
Black

Accent Colors

Curry
Teal
Fuchsia
Burgundy
Purple
Any and every offbeat color
All neons

Textures

Gauze
Heavy cotton
Wide wale corduroy
Cut velvet
Suede
Rayon
Burlap
Ribbed knits
Challis (rayon)
Leather
Any coarsely textured fabric

Accessories as Your Trademark

This is where Arty's emphasis should be. Your free and easy clothes desperately need a focal point—a strong pendant necklace or, even better, a belt with a big wide buckle that gives you form and silhouette and brings control to your flamboyance.

Get several interesting belts, the kind that rest on your hips. Look for metallic textures, brightly colored entwined ropes, even a belt that jangles a little for fun. These keep your look together.

Earrings should be big and important (preferably not small and dangling, because that's what you'd be expected to wear)—strong Egyptian bronze, for example, to bring the focus to your face.

Bags can run the gamut from huge carryalls or a railroad conductor's bag to a tiny shoulder bag just big enough to hold essentials.

The danger for you is overaccessorizing. Nobody can be expected to balance minis and maxis with hip belts, scarves and boots, colors and textures, and dangling earrings—all your traditional favorites.

Remember to bring focus and control to your look by being very selective in your choice of accessories. If you don't wear a belt, focus with a strong necklace, or compensate with bold earrings. Whatever you do, remember to have only one major focal point—that's your personal rule for accessorizing—because you're most likely to be wearing complicated layers.

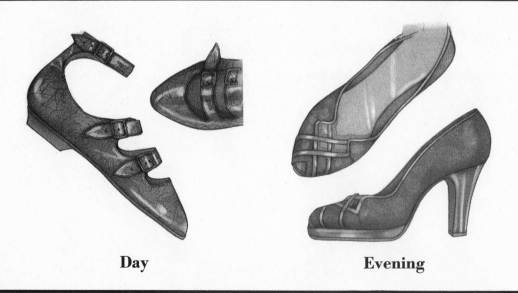

Day   **Evening**

Arty-Offbeat Accessories

The Bag

Basic

Basic

Basic

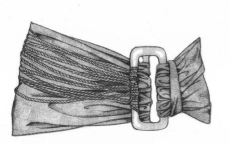

Creative

Creative

Creative

Summary

As an Arty-Offbeat, you probably feel you're the freest spirit of them all—and so you may be—but there's always the chance that you aren't taking as much advantage of that freedom as you could, that you're narrowing your choices in ways you may not even notice. You can be so intent on being the essence of Arty-Offbeat in every respect, every detail, that you miss the full range of adventure that's open to you within your image parameters. It's a big wide exhilarating world between those boundaries, and it's all yours if you make the most of both the Basic and the Creative.

Most of the time you dress in dark, murky colors. If you experiment with primary or neon colors, it's to use them as accents—never to wear a whole outfit of them. You're very fond of layers, lots of layers, though once in a while you'll risk wearing only one. For you, boots and bold textured hose are a staple in every season, though occasionally you'll wear shoes and solid hose instead. For Artys who are into Punk, legwear is insistently the focus of each outfit. On those rare occasions you allow your legwear to blend in, it's another instance of what on someone else is Basic, on you is Creative because it's the less expected. Though what you wear is mostly craft jewelry, now and then you'll go so far as to borrow a wide silver cuff from Exotic.

Arty-Offbeats tend to be trendy, but too trendy can veer into punk. Too trendy can even become a habit, which is the very opposite of creative. For you as an Arty-Offbeat, adapting more to society's style may be the really creative thing to do because it's so unexpected.

You're almost instinctively "anti-outfit"—probably because you think an "outfit" by its very nature, especially if planned by someone else, can't express your originality. But what makes Arty original is not dressing in bits and pieces—however striking or unusual each piece may be. Originality is pulling the pieces together for a total look that's uniquely you.

Of all the image types, you may be the most independent in the way you think and the way you look. Yet independence, when it becomes automatic, can turn into rigidity, and that can narrow your options, keep you hemmed into a small corner of the world when you could lay claim to so much more.

If you changed your mind-set even a little, your natural creativity would open up all sorts of areas you've never probed before. And you'd feel recharged because you tried something new. The aim is not to abandon your true image, not to try to be somebody else, but to tap all the possibilities deep inside you, especially those that allow you entrance to the Big World. Being true to yourself, your best, doesn't have to lock you out of that world. Your best has more potential than you have ever realized. Perhaps the real test of your creativity is how appropriately you can express your individuality, to be truly welcomed in that larger world, and become a valuable part of it.

6

If You're a

FEMININE-ROMANTIC

If you scored more E's than any other letter, you're a Feminine-Romantic, a sister-under-the-skin of such women as:

Jaclyn Smith	*Crystal Gayle*
Jane Seymour	*Liv Ullman*
Meryl Streep	*Rosalynn Carter*
Mia Farrow	*Peggy Fleming*

If you are a Feminine-Romantic, the key word for you is "soft." Soft of look, soft of skin, soft of manner, soft of heart—but *not* soft of head.

Men love you. You always make them feel more masculine, more protective. Everything about you is soft and friendly, sometimes even shy. You're coquettish without trying to be. Men see you as close to being their perfect female because you're so pretty and sweet. The girl next door . . . the girl they want to marry and protect.

Your life-style is "homemade"; your natural habitat, contrived chaos. Your room always has a slightly rumpled, lived-in look. You prefer Victorian furnishings whether the setting is modern or old. You never throw anything away.

You always see yourself wearing pastels and soft fabrics. You never wear black unless it's velvet or taffeta. You choose skirts over pants because skirts are more feminine—and dresses over all else because they are the most feminine. You're never sexy, obvious, blatant, or aggressive. (If your blouse button is open, it appears to be a mistake.) You'll choose sashes over belts, pearls over gold, pale blue over electric blue.

Your clothes all have a "little girl" look to them, demure high necklines in lace or with soft bows and sheer fabrics. You put femininity over chic. You love a Victorian look. You enjoy looking pristine, but you wouldn't dream of having a "touch-me-not" air. Your clothing never looks starched or crisp. You prefer a sash to a belt, a flower to a pin, a ribbon to a chain. Soft full skirts and poet blouses pulled together with wide, crushy sashes are your look. You'll never wear a really short skirt to show your legs. You know you can show them off to much better advantage simply by sitting down and crossing them in a very feminine way.

You never look "made-up." Natural, but softly radiant, is the look you aim for. Your hair always looks soft, never "set."

As a Feminine-Romantic, your most likely mistake is to look too "little girl," too unimportant. There comes a time when you'd do better to tone down the ruffles and switch to a more sophisticated cowl neckline. You should trust your feminine essence to show through even chic clothes. As it is, opening your closet door would probably reveal the following:

Colors and Combinations	Primarily pale, pastel, and especially pink
	Also, a great deal of white
Fabrics and Textures	Anything as long as it's soft—silk, velvet, batiste, angora, wool crepe, voile
	Nothing crisp, starchy, standoffish
Patterns	Small Victorian florals, gingham checks, thin stripes, plain soft solids
Accessories	Very little jewelry, usually fragile and light—small pearl earrings, a demure gold locket
	Crushy belts and sashes in soft pastels
	A silk flower on a velvet choker

As for your shopping patterns, there's one word for them: haphazard. You're impulsive. If you see it and like it, you'll buy it. That's why you often have no top for a bottom piece—a skirt, say—you fell in love with. Because your favorite colors are white and pastels, and they appear most in spring and summer, that's when you do most of your buying. For seasonal updates you look to jabots, soft sashes, or camisoles whenever available. You'll find them in charmeuse for winter, cotton lace for summer. In the fall, you scout for antique jewelry and pearls at estate sales.

How do you come out as a Feminine-Romantic? Your pluses are clear: you're appealing, warm, loving, and feminine to the core. Your minuses are that you're not taken seriously when you need and want to be, and that unadulterated femininity can come across as a ploy, more than the real thing. All in all, clothes that help you evolve from "little-girl" feminine to "grown-up" feminine can make that natural appeal even more irresistible, as you'll see in the following pages.

Clothes for the Feminine-Romantic

Basic and Creative

Note: When you look at the illustrations that follow, be sure to keep in mind that Basic means essentially "expected" for that type, and Creative means a looser, "less-expected" interpretation.

For the Feminine-Romantic, the "expected" is skirts at all times, no jackets, flowing lines, body-skimming fit, softer fabrics, pastel colors, and an overall sweetly feminine look.

The looser, "less expected" interpretation consists of more tailored skirts, jackets at least sometimes, stronger lines, more structured fit, fabrics with more body, deeper colors, and a generally more grown-up look.

Dressing for Your Job

Most jobs, especially those that lead to higher levels, call for looking—and being—competent and adult. This is the most difficult area for you because though your foremost concern has to be getting the proper respect on the job, getting that respect is normally something you don't want to address head-on.

The secret is to combine femininity and authority. They're not necessarily a contradiction in terms. The outfits shown here don't shortchange femininity, but they don't undermine authority either. When you learn to achieve that balance, you'll enjoy a stronger sense of yourself in both your private life and the workplace.

Dressing for Your Home Life

Home is the place where you not only can, but should, give your skirts some time off. These days, skirts—no matter how loose and casual they may be—still look a little more "proper" than pants. (Sometimes even prissy when you should look more comfortable.)

Trousers should be a part of every woman's life-style today, especially at home, where comfort and relaxed style are primary. Easy pants-dressing brings Feminine into the real world of comfort and leisure.

In pants, whether you're hostess or guest, you instantly look like an active participant in today's sporty life-style. And the delightful paradox is, it's pants that seem to bring out your femininity best. Seeing you in pants is totally disarming—everybody loves it!

Dressing for Your Social Life

Being feminine is such a charming thing to be, you might believe you shouldn't have to dress any way beyond—like "grown-up" or "appropriate" or "important." But there's nothing in feminine that says you can't be grown-up *and* feminine, appropriate *and* feminine, or even important *and* feminine. If you think there is, it's only in your head. What you're probably thinking—without even realizing it—is that you don't want to look old, or settled. And you needn't, as you'll see if you study the outfits that follow. All are as feminine as can be, but still grown-up and effective.

Dressing for Your Job

Administrative Level

Basic

Ruffled blouse and straight skirt for femininity—these are the elements of her favorite office uniform. Special touches to underline her femininity are the crushy wide belt and the soft bows on her shoes. The source of her basic security? That cascade of ruffles and the nipped-in waist. The end result? A soft, but important, first step toward looking professional.

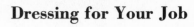

Dressing for Your Job

Administrative Level

Creative

The look here is a dress that's "finished," feminine style. The mark of extra effort: the shawl that wraps it up. Did she take a gamble? 'Deed she did—*no frills.* The overall effect? A cleanness of line, a more grown-up look.

Basic

The classic feminine shirtwaist, the beloved perennial that never fades from the scene no matter what the fashion crop of the day is. Here the special touches that make it up-to-the-minute are a contrasting bow, chain belt, and cuff links. The basic security stems from femininity reaffirmed in the sweetness of the bow, the soft texture of the knit. The essential impact? A one-time little girl turned professional.

Dressing for Your Job

Managerial Level

Creative

A sweater becomes a fashion statement for Feminine for a look that's still appropriate for work. The big draped bow of the sweater, strong yet feminine, makes it important enough to stand alone. Long pleats balance the bow and add the fashion detail to pull the pieces together. The end result? Separates that function as well as a dress, in a far more casual way.

Dressing for Your Job

Executive Level

Basic *

The classic Chanel-type suit in a distinctly feminine version. The soft texture and pastel color are special touches deliberately chosen to offset the severity of a suit. And for a Feminine-Romantic, basic security is well bolstered by the femininity of a bow, the pearls, and the graceful, delicate shoes. The end result? A striking assertion of power and confidence in an ultra-feminine mode.

* On the Executive Level a suit is always Basic and universally respected in the working world. (It's no longer seen as an attempt to imitate men.) Your personal choice of suit shape and how you accessorize it are what make it individual and right for your image-type.

Dressing for Your Home Life

Weeknights After Work

*Creative**

Feminine softness in a jumpsuit—it's not only possible, it's terrific. And it doesn't take a lot of effort, just a little courage— the courage to put appropriate comfort first for a change. For Feminine, pants may be truly daring; the surprise will be how truly feminine she feels in them. The overall effect? Her mirror will tell her the truth: A jumpsuit can be every bit as feminine as a skirt!

* At home, the jumpsuit is the one category that pushes against the parameters of each image-type in exactly the way each type needs it the most. For Sport, Classic, and Feminine a jumpsuit is Creative; for Exotic, Arty, and Sexy, it's Basic.

Dressing for Your Home Life

Weekend Dressing

Basic

The essence of this look is the pants suit at its softest—and with all the special touches that are the hallmarks of femininity: the lacy collar, the flower, the ribbon. For Feminine, the basic security here is the softness of a knit. The overall effect? The epitome of femininity in a pants suit.

Dressing for Your Home Life

Weekend Dressing

Creative

The look here is that of a little girl grown up. The special effort made to achieve it shows up in a number of ways. For once, Feminine is *not* wearing a dress. She's using a strong fashion accessory—the patterned waist-wrap, chicly tied—and she's finished the look with the right accessories. Is she taking a risk? For a Feminine she certainly is. She's daring to be a sophisticated woman, in pants. And the risk pays off in an "I'll take care of you" self-confidence, instead of the usual "You take care of me" plea.

Dressing for Your Social Life

Cocktail Party

Basic

The quintessentially feminine look of a soft, fluttery cocktail dress. One special touch of the unexpected is the omitting of a necklace so that her face is framed only by the lace. Her basic security is well taken care of by the soft fullness of flowing sleeves and the sashed ribbon waist. The overall effect? A clear statement that, for this female, Feminine wins over Chic.

Dressing for Your Social Life

Cocktail Party

Creative

For Feminine, the definitive suit: structured, stylized lace. Softness held to the
minimum attests to the extra effort made
here. A stiffened blouse is turned into a
jacket, and with that effort, she takes an
unaccustomed risk of being in command,
showing confidence. The overall effect?
Feminine *in control.*

Dressing for Your Social Life

Casual Evenings at a Friend's

Basic

The look is casual layers, but in feminine mode rather than sporty. Special touches: big full sleeves, lace-edged; the tiny floral print of her underskirt. Her basic security stems from being and looking what she truly is: frankly feminine with a dash of fashion. The overall effect? American country feminine at its most appealing.

Dressing for Your Social Life

Casual Evenings at a Friend's

Creative

Here the special fizz is femininity-plus-fun.
Indications of the extra effort put in are:
going to a longer length of skirt to work
with tied-up sandals, and balancing the
whole with dolman sleeves. The risk for
Feminine? The outfit is as strong on fashion as it is on femininity, but the end result is more than worth it—feminine
separates of easy sophistication.

Dressing for Your Social Life

Dinner at a Fine Restaurant

The look here is Feminine "grown up." There's nothing little-girl about that laced-up, wide-U plunging neckline. But by her very nature, Feminine will venture into sophistication only so far. In the end, her instinct for propriety prevails and to feel more secure, more "herself," she softens the unaccustomed nakedness with a cameo on a ribbon choker. That choker—and her upswept wispy hair—bring the focus to her face, yet the low neckline still counts. The overall effect? Femininity with a new dimension: excitement!

These examples of Basic and Creative dressing for the Feminine-Romantic have been deliberately chosen to point up the contrast as sharply as possible in order to make it clear how wide a choice is open to you—*within the parameters of your type.* The pieces of the minimal wardrobe that follow fall somewhere in the middle. By definition, a minimal wardrobe has to give you the most generally useful and basic pieces you need to start with. Once you have these, once your "center" is covered—so to speak—you're free to extend your wardrobe with as many of the more purely Basic or Creative elements as you want, so long as they are *within your type.*

Minimal Wardrobe for the Feminine-Romantic

1. Cream cashmere jacket

2. Mauve mohair tweed sweater

3. Mauve sheer linen blouse

4. Cream silk blouse

5. Pink tissue taffeta blouse

6. Mauve rabbit hair skirt

7. Pearl gray wool crepe skirt

8. Purple velvet dress

9. Mauve silk dress

10. Lace jabot

11. Gray suede belt

12. Gray suede pouch bag

13. Gray suede shoes

14. Pearl earrings

15. Necklace

Colors and Textures for the Feminine-Romantic

Most women were raised on traditional feminine colors. Gentle blues, face-powder pinks, softly glowing apricots, and pristine white to point up the softness.

As a Feminine-Romantic, to hostess a luncheon you would most likely choose a delicate apricot silk dress with ruffles—a soft, unthreatening color to enhance your femininity. You never care about what is in fashion, or in the stores. You cling to all the old-fashioned values of femininity. The color and style of everything you wear have a softening, calming effect on those around you. You're never a threat . . . always easy to be with.

Though almost every woman would love to get away with pink, you're the only one who always can—for any and every event. For going to a concert, your pink dress would be your uniform—and look like anything but. Pink, in fact, is your "little black dress."

Core Colors	*Accent Colors*	*Textures*	
White	Pink	Lace	Cotton
Cream	Dusty rose	Voile	Tissue linen
Mauve	Lilac	Silk	Angora
Pearl gray	Pale yellow	Cashmere	Sheer wool
Apricot	Mint green	Rayon	Crepe
Purple	Dusty blue	Chiffon	Organza
		Velvet	

Accessories as Your Trademark

Accessories don't loom large in your scheme of things. You probably own and wear very little jewelry. It might be the locket your boyfriend gave you for your birthday, or pearls your husband chose as an anniversary gift. If you like to shop, you'll pick up pretty flower petal earrings or a necklace of heart charms. Soft colors melt you, and you have a modest collection of fabric sashes in soft lavender, rose, mint green, and the like.

Since your look is rather pale and fragile—in makeup and in clothes—your jewelry can't be too bold and strong. But Feminine shouldn't mean colorless or unsophisticated. It doesn't even mean jewelry all the time.

Consider a real gardenia on a ribbon tied around your neck instead of pearls, a soft scarf around your head instead of earrings, and for once, a lace ascot instead of a bow at your neck.

Accessories are often a subtle clue to more than just your taste. They can indicate how far along you are in your development, whether you still see yourself as a "little girl" because you're fond of all things feminine and sweet and precious, or whether you think being a feminine woman has its own special kind of power.

When you choose a blouse for your suit, try a gutsier lace-trimmed linen instead of soft embroidered silk. If you need a belt for that fabulous new dress, make it a stronger-contrast wide suede belt instead of a pastel scarf belt. When it comes to jewelry, be sure it makes a statement.

You'll better define your image with choices like the following:

Feminine-Romantic Accessories

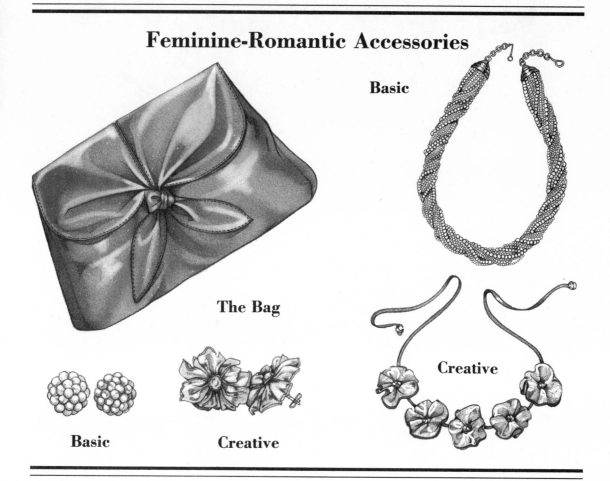

Basic

The Bag

Creative

Basic

Creative

Creative

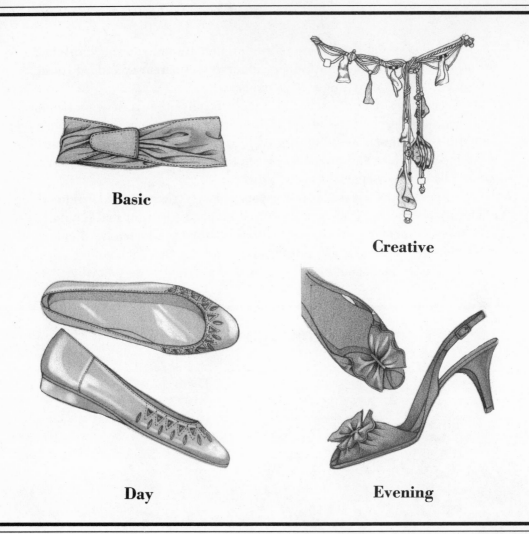

Basic

Creative

Day

Evening

Summary

The clothes you've seen in this chapter should give you some idea of how much you can make of your Feminine-Romantic image no matter where you are or what you're doing. Each outfit has been chosen to meet the standard all your clothes should meet: first, to be right for your image; second, to be right for the occasion; third, to be right for your body. But these are only a sampling.

Now you're ready to strike deep into the whole wide range of choices that are open to you. Whether you choose Basic or Creative, you can enjoy all the variety without the worry, because whatever you choose will be right, as long as it's within the parameters of your image-type.

As a Feminine-Romantic, you're almost always likely to prefer a dress, but sometimes you'll opt for separates. Most of the time, you'd rather wear a sweater than a structured jacket, but once in a while you may find yourself willing to go with more authoritative structure. For dress-up occasions, your first love may be sheer chiffon with a delicate floral all-over print. One day you might surprise everyone (including yourself) by choosing a soft solid-color silk—not in your usual pastels but in soft khaki, pumpkin, or pearl gray. You're just naturally drawn to flared, bias-cut skirt lines, but you may find you feel every bit as feminine in silk flare pants. Chances are, your all-time favorite sweater is an angora turtleneck. An open-weave, V-neck cotton sweater could provide femininity with a new twist.

Though you may feel nothing says Feminine like full billowing sleeves, there might come a day when you'll find out bare arms can have their own special appeal. While you usually find it hard to resist embroidery and smocking because it's so girlish, you might learn to adore draped necklines. Your first choice may always be high-heeled sandals, but for authoritative femininity, nothing beats your first pair of smart closed pumps.

Your favorite belt may be crushed suede cinching your waist. For up-to-the-minute femininity, you might rely on a soft leather hip belt. When it comes to jewelry, you may depend on pearls, cameos, diamond studs—all real, of course. But now and again you can treat yourself to a piece of modern jewelry, even if it's not so precious—as long as it accents your femininity.

If you've always had long hair, which you consider the essence of femininity, short curly hair might be a delightful surprise for you. It's every bit as feminine—and a lot more carefree. As for makeup, you can go on with the pale delicate shades you've always loved or try stronger, seasonal colors and discover they only heighten your femininity.

Most Feminine-Romantics are glad to be exactly what they are. If, just once, you'd like to admit that under all that femininity there's a healthy streak of female sexuality, you can make your next soft sweater a plunging V-neck instead of the usual jewelneck. It isn't a big step, but it could get you big results—not only in how people look at you, but in how you look at yourself.

The goal you're aiming for is not to be a different image-type from what you are, but to be your best self within your image-type. And your best self means your most varied, most widely ranged self. Centered, yes, but not limited. True to yourself, but free to be *all* of your self.

7

If You're a

SEXY-ALLURING

If you scored more F's than any other letter, you're a Sexy-Alluring. And you're charged with the special magnetism that radiates from such women as:

Raquel Welch	*Dolly Parton*
Victoria Principal	*Morgan Fairchild*
Ann-Margret	*Suzanne Somers*
Joan Collins	*Bernadette Peters*

Since you're a Sexy-Alluring, your best friend is your body. You're proud of it, and love to use it to every advantage.

You prefer men to women, which is not surprising since men often prefer you to other women. And the men always respond. Women are more likely to be curious, and critical. Some women may think the Sexy type went out with Marilyn Monroe, but you know better. Sexiness is not a fashion, and it doesn't go out of style.

You may live in a sleek, contemporary apartment with lots of white, chrome, and glass. But when it comes to how you live, your earthy sexiness can't be bound down to anything too sleek or strict. Hence, friends who really know you aren't surprised to find that neatness and perfect grooming don't rate high on your list of concerns.

When it comes to health and beauty, you want to keep your body looking as good as possible for as long as possible. You're not as fanatic about your face, though you use lots of makeup: always generous amounts of eyeshadow, blush, and lipstick—makeup that *has* to be glamorous. Your hair is probably long, and as full as it can be—usually styled to hang over your face, on one side or both. You count on your hair for glamour.

People see you as superconfident. Most of them don't know anyone else who would dare to show off her body so boldly. Actually, you may be quite insecure, but insecure about yourself as a person, not as a female.

Men are crazy about you. They're delighted to be seen with you on social occasions "with the guys." But they may hesitate when it comes to business appearances. Women are conflicted over you. They'd like to have your success with men, but they wouldn't be willing to take the risks they think you do.

In matters of dress, your body determines your clothing. If you're an executive, you cover and camouflage your curves—in this instance they can be a detriment. If you're not in a conservative job, you play with clothes, let them follow the lines of your body in fluid jersey knits, short straight skirts—fashion is secondary to cling.

You attract with your clothing, it points up your body and that gives you confidence. One look inside your closet would show where your heart, and your instincts, lie.

Colors and Combinations	Red is No. 1; but any other color will do as long as it's vibrant, shocking, or intense—preferably all three
Patterns	Dramatic florals, riveting prints
Textures	Fluid jerseys, clingy knits, thin suedes, silks, satins
	Everything crushable, invitingly so; hardly anything crisp
Accessories	First and foremost, big and bold: smashing belts—usually wide; necklaces—plunging pendants and bib collars

When it comes to shopping, you're a "spotter"—you'll see an item that will show off your figure and you'll buy it. You don't "pull together" a wardrobe. If you see a great waist cinch in gold leather, you'll buy it, and worry about combinations later.

For special occasions, whatever the event, you feel you need something "sensational." You'll go low-cut jersey, or strapless and form-fitting whenever you can. If it *has* to be corporate or chic, it's usually black.

At holiday time, your best season, you'll pick up a sexy beaded or sequin top and wear it with black cropped tapered pants. You'll buy high heels—or strappy, high-heeled sandals—in brilliant colors to change a look. You're up on legwear, patterned, jeweled, or ultra-sheer for evening to focus on your legs.

Up to now, if you've traded style for the sexy look you love, it's probably because you didn't realize the two can be combined—and quite successfully. You may have slipped into buying lower quality for what seemed like good reasons—sexy clothes were less expensive, and for you, quality was secondary—and this way you thought you could have more clothes.

Perhaps you haven't understood the power of subtle colors. You've been so intent on standing out, your clothes have become your personality, your entire statement. The way you dress overshadows everything else about you—except your sexiness.

The pluses of your image stand out loud and clear. You're just naturally exciting to men (and that's *most* men!); you're warm and vivacious and full of life, you're sure of yourself as a woman, and very happy about it.

The minuses are equally apparent. You're a little too eager for attention . . . likely to be too dressy as a result (just as Sporty-Casual often makes the opposite mistake of underdressing). You're too willing to sacrifice quality for impact because you haven't yet discovered it doesn't have to be a case of "either/or." You can have them both—as you'll see in the following pages.

Clothes for the Sexy-Alluring

Basic and Creative

Note: When you scan the following illustrations remember that Basic means essentially "expected" for that type; and Creative means a looser, "less-expected" interpretation.

For the Sexy-Alluring, the "expected" is clinging skirts, short fitted jackets, slinky lines, body-hugging fit, sensuous fabrics, daring colors, and always a look-at-me look.

The looser, "less-expected" interpretation consists of flared skirts, easy unconstructed jackets, fluid lines, eased fit, quality fabrics, more subdued colors, and generally an aura of more refinement.

Dressing for Your Job

The sexy look doesn't have to contradict the professional look—though you have to be cautious that it doesn't. Your look is automatically the least respected on the job. Wouldn't it be a shame to lose out on job advancement because of too much body exposure? You don't have to let that happen.

Care enough to tone down whatever looks obvious. Leave the clinging, slinky fabrics, the low-cut necklines, the too-high heels at home. Look for well-tailored fabrics that have body. Take one step of structure over what you would instinctively choose—instead of draped crepe, pick soft wool; instead of sheer silk, raw silk. And wear a blouse under most suits.

Learn to judge yourself as you would judge other women. If you wouldn't hire yourself in a certain outfit, don't wear it.

Dressing for Your Home Life

For you, one of the most delicious pleasures of being at home is you know you don't have to be "on" all the time. You can relax and be comfortable, even to the point of covering up your wonderful legs in pants.

Home is where your sex appeal doesn't have to be always on call. It's private time for you, and there's no audience you need to please or impress. Not that you need to worry about that. Your sexiness is never far from the surface—and you can't hide it easily.

On you, even a baggy loose sweater looks sexy because your sexiness is as much psychological as it is physical—it's a matter of attitude above all.

Dressing for Your Social Life

This is your favorite area—you live to shine in it, and you do. Whether the occasion is blue-jeans informal or black-tie formal, your sexiness is never in question. What may be a matter for judgment is your subtlety. Even when you're basking in the glow of that sexiness, people need to be reassured that you have your priorities straight, that you put them, and the occasion, ahead of the need to show how sexy you are. Just turn the page to see sexy-alluring clothes for a total life-style.

Dressing for Your Job

Administrative Level

Basic

The look here is proof that *conservative* sweater-dressing is possible for Sexy. The special touch that underlines the surprise: *neatness.* Her basic security is still very comfortingly there, though—in a knit that's close to her body and shows lots of leg. The overall effect? A respectable version of her beloved sexy knit.

Dressing for Your Job

Administrative Level

Creative

This is knit dressing in a looser mode. The dolman sleeve, which doesn't show the body, is the mark of extra effort (the mark of fashion, too). The daring risk for Sexy in this outfit is that it's a more subtle way to show her curves . . . even hide them for work. The end result? Sexy in softened noncling.

Basic

The true-to-type sheath dress, short and clingy—a signature look for Sexy. The special touches here are the simple stylized collar, the tailored handbag, all sending the same message: control. The security that underlies her confidence is the happily familiar close-to-the-body cut. The overall effect? Authoritative, but still permissibly sexy.

Dressing for Your Job

Managerial Level

Creative

This, a much easier dress shape, is a newer, bigger look with flow. The signs of extra effort are shading sexiness into femininity, with softness of dress and belt, simplicity of accessories. Sexy's willingness to take a risk is signaled by less show of leg, to come across as less aggressive, more feminine. The end result is a more current and adaptable dress.

Dressing for Your Job

Executive Level

Basic *

The look: the sexy executive suit, efficient
and crisp, but still figure-revealing. The
special touches that underline the whole
effect are: the formality of a men's wear
pinstripe; the masculine belt, defining a
tiny waist; the deliberate omission of jewelry. The basic security that underlies it
all: Sexy can still count on showing off her
figure with the fitted small jacket and
short straight skirt. And her strippy high-
heels accent lots of leg. The overall effect? Exactly what she wants: clearly authoritative . . . clearly sexy.

* On the Executive Level a suit is always Basic
and universally respected in the working world.
(It's no longer seen as an attempt to imitate the
male.) Your personal choice of suit shape and
how you accessorize it are what make it individual
and right for your image-type.

Dressing for Your Home Life

Weeknights After Work

*Basic**

Three little words sum up the look here: glamour that's comfortable. But caring doesn't take time off. It shows in the extra attention focused on accessories. The gamble for Sexy: a rather loose silhouette that telegraphs innocence rather than experience. And what does it all add up to? Relaxed sexiness that could go from poolside to party.

* At home, the jumpsuit is the one category that pushes against the parameters of each image-type in exactly the way each type needs it the most. For Sporty, Classic, and Feminine a jumpsuit is Creative; for Exotic, Arty, and Sexy, it's Basic.

Dressing for Your Home Life

Weekend Dressing

Basic

If ever there was a standard classic in sexiness, this is it: a plunging sweater over
tight pants. The special touches can be
summed up in two words: everything
clings. The basics of Sexy security are
very much in evidence—the softness of
her angora sweater and velvet pants, the
height of her heels. The unmistakable
message? Confident acknowledgment that
her body is terrific.

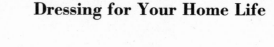

Dressing for Your Home Life

Weekend Dressing

Creative

This look is another standard classic of sexiness, but softer: the loose, big sweater over pants. Which doesn't mean Sexy is trying less hard, just that she's channeling her efforts in a different direction . . . using the sweater not as a body statement but as a fashion statement, which means less show of body curves. Yet that's a gamble she's willing to take because what she wins in overall effect is a little less aggressive, but a little more glamorous, sexiness.

Dressing for Your Social Life

Cocktail Party

Basic

The slip dress is Sexy's basic dress-up uni-form—hers since the beginning of time. Here, for once, she's willing to let the drama of the print share equal billing with her body. Deliberately unadorned, her body is a blank canvas, letting her dress have its fullest impact.

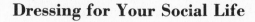

Dressing for Your Social Life

Cocktail Party

Creative

The look here is sexiness as drama. And all signs are Go: long, tight sleeves; open-to-the-waist back; above-the-knee skirt. Everything is aimed at underwriting the ultimate gamble: maximum body display. The overall effect? High-octane sexiness in more subtle exposure.

Dressing for Your Social Life

Casual Evenings at a Friend's

Basic

This is the look of conventional sexiness, what everybody expects of a Sexy-Alluring, including herself. Even the special touches are the classics for Sexy: a slightly see-through top, a short skirt. And her basic security comes from the primary expectation: a body-hugging silhouette. The end result is exactly what all the above is meant to lead up to: attention-getting body display.

Dressing for Your Social Life

Casual Evenings at a Friend's

Creative

Relaxed sexiness is deliberately arrived at with careful planning. The results of the extra effort are pants instead of a skirt and an uncinched top. The loose silhouette and, for once, hiding her legs proves that Sexy is willing to take a risk when it's worthwhile. The end result? Sexiness that's low-key but unmistakable, without trying too hard.

Dressing for Your Social Life

Dinner at a Fine Restaurant

The core of the look here is unmistakable sexuality under cool rein. The familiar trademarks of the Sexy-Alluring are very much in evidence: the sophisticated shape, the wrapped waist, the plunging neckline. But there's a difference: unexpected restraint, most noticeable in her sculptured hairdo and her choice of only one accessory—glamorous swinging earrings. The final tally? Sexy can be elegant without losing one watt of electricity.

These examples of Basic and Creative dressing for the Sexy-Alluring have been deliberately chosen to point up the contrast as sharply as possible in order to make it clear how wide a choice is open to you—*within the parameters of your type.* The pieces of the minimal wardrobe that follow fall somewhere in the middle. By definition, a minimal wardrobe has to give you the most useful and basic pieces you need to start with. Once you have these, once your "center" is covered, you're free to extend your wardrobe with as many of the more purely Basic and Creative elements as you want, so long as they are *within your type.*

Minimal Wardrobe for the Sexy-Alluring

1. Black wool jersey jacket

2. Red wool crepe jacket

9. Red jersey dress

3. Red jersey top

4. White charmeuse blouse

5. Shocking pink angora sweater

8. White wool crepe pants

6. Black wool jersey skirt

7. Purple suede skirt

11. Black suede bag

12.

10. Black belt

14. Earrings

13. Black shoes

Stockings, point d'esprit

15. Necklace

155

Colors and Textures for the Sexy-Alluring

Sexy loves red but also pink and white (if they're charmeuse) and gold and silver. And, of course, Sexy couldn't do without black.

Actually, if you're a Sexy, fit is more important to you than color. You want color simple and basic enough so it doesn't compete with your assets—or distract from whichever part of your body you intend to accentuate. That's why you don't like prints, they distract from your body.

For you, color always has to be judged in combination with fabric. The more attention-getting the fabric, the more subdued your color should be—shocking pink in silk versus face-powder pink in charmeuse. For a high-intensity occasion, for example a premiere, you might choose a shocking pink silk, and add to the dazzle. But for a dinner at a lovely restaurant with friends, face-powder pink in charmeuse would blend more appropriately.

Core Colors

White
Shocking pink
Turquoise
Emerald green
Electric blue
Red
Purple
Black

Accent Colors

Face-powder pink
Peach
Mint green
Chartreuse
Silver
Gold

Textures

Silk
Angora
Knits
Wool crepe
Lamé
Satin
Rayon
Wool jersey
Suede
Sequins

Accessories as Your Trademark

As a Sexy-Alluring, you're well aware that bare skin is one of your greatest assets. Yet more often than not, you'll go overboard on accessories—as if you're afraid bare, beautiful skin won't be enough. You tend to gravitate toward jewelry that's bigger and bolder than you need, to get attention—and you change it often for the same reason.

Actually, getting attention should be the least of your worries. That innate sexiness of yours will always get noticed. The jewelry and accessories you choose should be aimed at quietly enhancing it, not announcing it with brass bands and fireworks. Understatement in this area makes you that much more intriguing, more desirable.

So pass up the massive bib necklaces in favor of, perhaps, no necklace (that can be the sexiest). Put the bold noisy earrings away and let your face be the focus (and be especially careful not to wear too-dressy jewelry with a T-shirt and jeans). See what a low-slung belt instead of a wide cinch will do for your hips. And sometimes a neckline or the architecture of a dress can be sexier left completely unadorned and exposed. But, when only an accessory will do, make your choice from one of these:

Sexy-Alluring Accessories

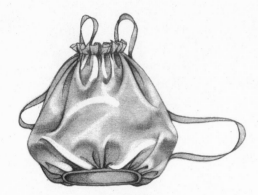

The Bag

Basic

Creative

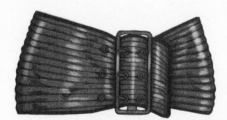

Basic

Creative

Basic

Creative

Day

Evening

Summary

The aim, so far, has been to show you (1) how crucial it is to decide what your particular image-type is; (2) how faithfully you can dress to that image-type in every area of your life; and (3) how much variety you can enjoy through Basic and Creative dressing within that type.

As a Sexy-Alluring, you need never feel constricted or hemmed in by the parameters of your image-type. There's a good deal of territory within those borders for you to explore, have fun with, and make the most of. The following are a few samples of the many choices you have. The more you experiment, the more will open up for you.

For Sexy-Alluring, tight, body-hugging clothes—a tight sweater-dress, for instance—are Basic. Loose, bias-cut satin or silk that falls against the body's curves, merely suggesting the whole shape, enliven your type. One of your favorite pieces may be a short, tight mini-skirt. Sooner or later, you'll discover that a longer, straight-line skirt with side slits may be even sexier. For glamorous occasions, your favorite outfit may be a cocktail dress with bare shoulders. For a change, you may want to try a covered-up cocktail dress with a high turtleneck.

You probably love glitzy fabrics for evening—gold or silver lamé, sequins, or beading. You might try a more subtle way of getting the same effect, for example, silver or gold charmeuse, or a vibrant print silk.

Chances are you seldom wear a jacket, but if you do, nine times out of ten, it'll be a fitted sweater-jacket. One fine day you'll choose a classic double-breasted, man-tailored jacket in cashmere wool.

Vibrant, attention-drawing colors—electric blue, shocking pink, pencil yellow, and the like—may be your particular favorites. More subtle colors—taupes, grays, cream, or soft pastels like peach, mint, and lavender—may look even sexier. You'll often want the sheen of satin; at other times only the subtlety of silk will do. You tend to gravitate toward solid colors, but you'll go for a print now and then, even if it doesn't show off your body as much as a solid would.

Depending on the occasion, you'll go to extremes with high-heeled strappy bare sandals—or even bare feet! In a more conservative mood, you'll decide on high-heeled closed pumps.

When you have a hankering for special notice, you'll count on a low-hanging pendant with large dangling earrings to bring attention to your face. When you want to be really subtle, you'll wear no jewelry at all.

Long hair—a veritable mane—swinging free at all times is what you really believe in. Once in a while you'll change to a soft pulled-back twist. Your nails are usually long and red, but, just for a change, you'll sometimes turn to clear nail polish.

Most of the time you insist on a finished perfect makeup, but on occasion you'll opt for a change to a less finished, more natural look.

If, as a Sexy-Alluring, you have a problem, it's not in your sexiness. *That* you feel comfortable with and know how to make the most of. It's only in the area of your life where sexiness doesn't—indeed, shouldn't—hold center stage that you tend to be a little unsure of yourself. And the more unsure you feel, the more you resort to sexiness to make you feel in control, which only intensifies the problem.

The solution is don't try to be something you aren't . . . don't try to change your image, or copy someone else's. (It doesn't work, and even if it did, you wouldn't be happy with yourself.) The most effective way to deal with the situation is to prevent its ever coming up. Learn to push against your parameters. Learn to widen the scope of your image-type so you can always draw on clothes that are appropriate—not just to your body and personality, but also to your life-style and the particular event, be it a benefit, a museum opening, or a job interview. When you feel you're appropriately dressed, you feel confident about the image you project, confident about yourself. And that's a magnetism that outdraws even sex.

8

CROSSOVER DRESSING

Once you've gotten into the swing of Basic and Creative dressing, once you've experienced the fun of it, you may be emboldened to go on to the next stage: indulging yourself in Crossovers.

Crossovers are ways of dressing that let you go beyond your image-type when the situation calls for it, or when you want to express different sides of your personality—in some cases, sides you may not even know you had.

In a very basic way, Crossovers are what you've been experimenting with since you were sixteen. As you felt yourself changing, growing up, you kept trying to express your new self in different kinds of clothes. You knew you'd done it when you finally reached the point when everybody said, "It's *you*!" at the very moment when you were thinking to yourself, "It's *me*!"

Crossovers allow you to grow in different ways. They're not just an impulse. They result from a real need for a fuller expression of the person you've become.

Most people start with a certain physical type, and their personality develops around that type. Other people's personality develops in spite of, or against, their physical type. Whichever is the case with you, you shouldn't feel locked into being only one type. Crossovers give you room to grow, to change, to enjoy, to fantasize. They can develop from all sorts of circumstances—and depending on how you handle them—they can run the gamut from the natural evolution to the stunning reversal. Every image-type can cross over to any other image-type as long as she's true to herself at the core.

But a Sporty-Casual will cross over to Exotic-Dramatic, for instance, in a way that's different from the way a Feminine-Romantic would, or a Classic-Elegant. In each case, the end result is definitely Exotic, yet there's no loss of her own identity. Study the examples that follow and you'll see for yourself.

Sporty → Classic-Elegant

The Situation: You're a financial planner scheduled to have lunch with a wealthy client and her friends.

The Problem: You can't go to a fine restaurant in your usual casual skirt and top. You won't fit in with your client's friends, because they will think you're not on their level.

The Crossover Solution: A pretty gray silk dress worn with the familiar blazer jacket but in white, crisp (not wrinkled) linen. This is a basic Classic look you can feel comfortable with because it's not too far from your usual look, yet you haven't settled for wearing your "safe" practical jacket. If you wanted to venture further into a creative Classic, you'd choose a gabardine coatdress in cream or taupe.

Sporty → Exotic

The Situation: You've been invited to a cast party after rehearsals of the Joffrey Ballet.

The Problem: You don't want to come across as square, preppy, too regular or conservative. You'd like to blend in, at least this once, with these Exotic types. This is a tough crossover for you, so do it in the swiftest and easiest way.

The Crossover Solution: Do it with accessories. Start with a clear canvas—a simple off-white dress—and add a strong Exotic choker or a bib necklace. You might also try a low-slung wide leather hip belt, and then top it with a big-shoulder jacket—with pushed-up sleeves and nipped-in waist.

Sporty → Arty

The Situation: You've decided to take art lessons at the Art Student's League. It's very casual there—everybody knows everybody.

   The Problem: You'd very much like to be accepted—your class-mates look like such an interesting mix of people. You want to look re-laxed and current, and not too stiff. Besides, an easier image would hint at more creativity.

   The Crossover Solution: Exchange your classic campshirt for a boatneck top of crinkled cotton that hangs loose, with no collar, no but-tons. Instead of your straight khaki skirt, wear cropped pants or stirrup pants. Anchor and focus the look with a hip belt, softer, stringy, and dangling—even fabric or gauze wrapped around the waist—for a more Arty look. Wear sandals and the total look is Instant Careless. (If your hair is in a sharp exact line, loosen it for a freer version of your own style, even if you have to use styling mousse.)

Sporty → Feminine

The Situation: You've met a gentleman who arouses the most surprising feelings in you . . . a man you actually want to *be feminine for.*

   The Problem: How does the Sporty you show your feminine side without feeling as if you're putting on an act?

   The Crossover Solution: Think "soft" instead of "crisp." A soft dress, soft color, soft pastel to medium tones, or a soft water-washed print. Silk, rayon, sheer linen—a fabric that moves and swings when you walk. Soft full sleeves with a top that is a bit bloused, not tightly tucked in. Softer accessories—pearls, ivory, porcelain. (But very little jewelry. Instead, wear a real flower.) Higher heels, open toes, sling-back shoes.

Sporty → Sexy

The Situation: You've met the most terrific man, one you just *can't* let get away.

   The Problem: This is the biggest switch of all for you—even tougher than the switch to Exotic—because you hate anything verging

Sporty → Sexy

The easy shape of the jacket is the essence of Sporty, but by daring to draw attention—through the sparkly glitter of jacket, the body-revealing cling of soft fabric—Sporty crosses over to Sexy.

on entrapment or guile. Just remember, he's the man *nobody* can let get away.

The Crossover Solution: Be happy that you've got such good legs! Make the most of them with sheer stockings, higher-heeled sandals, and a shorter-skirted dress instead of separates. For dress-up, try a clinging straight dress of soft heavy silk that shows your figure. (You have a good figure, you've just never shown it off.) For security and the finishing touch, top it with a glamorous beaded sweater-jacket, belted in around the waist. P.S. Buy all new underwear—lacy . . . red . . . black . . . whatever turns you on—to help you cross over to Sexy, even mentally.

Classic → Sporty

The Situation: As a class mother, you're asked to take your child's class to the museum with other class mothers, teachers, and kids.

The Problem: There will probably be a tiring bus ride with much milling around and nonstop uproar. You would like to make people comfortable with you, as well as be comfortable with yourself.

The Crossover Solution: Start with Sporty's fabrics, which are more easy-care. This way you won't need to worry about how or where you sit, or whether a child musses you up. Wear khaki pants and a campshirt (linen instead of cotton) tied in a soft knot at your waist instead of tucked in, giving a more nonchalant look. Opt for a big shoulder canvas pouch instead of your usual small clutch bag. Leave your Gucci walking shoes at home and put on canvas espadrilles instead. No real jewelry for this outing.

Classic → Exotic

The Situation: You're going to a big farewell party and you want to stand out.

The Problem: You want to be sure you're going to be remembered, so you want a look that's stylized and striking. Definitely unusual.

The Crossover Solution: Choose a black, bare-back, halter-neck dress. Wear your hair up, strict and stylized for a change, perhaps with a comb twisted in. Add sheer black stockings, and finish the look with red high-heeled pumps. Since you would normally wear black pumps with this outfit, red designer pumps are an instant signal that you've broken out of your usual mold.

Classic → Arty

The Situation: You've rented a house for the summer in an Arty community—a Woodstock sort of place devoted to the laid-back country life.

   The Problem: You can't look as perfect as you usually do. You not only can't, you really don't want to.

   The Crossover Solution: Make it impossible for you to be as uptight as you usually are. Go in for easy-care fabrics. Instead of crisp, choose slightly wrinkled. Have your jumpsuit not in your usual gabardine, but in wrinkleable cotton—with a drawstring waistband instead of a fitted one, or possibly with no waistband at all, just belted at the hip. Skip your usual color palette of cream and taupe and change to curry and khaki. Pare your accessories down to as few as possible. A belt with a small pouch is accessory enough for Classic going to Arty. Instead of Arty's thong sandals, wear ankle-tied sandals. As for jewelry, you wouldn't, *couldn't*, wear Arty's jewelry, so don't wear any.

Classic → Feminine

The Situation: Your friends are giving you a party for your fiftieth birthday.

   The Problem: Your clothes are just plain older-looking, for the most part, because they're of such good quality, so *responsible*-looking. Now that that landmark birthday is almost here, you'd like to try a little softness, femininity—even youth—for the big event.

   The Crossover Solution: There's nothing more feminine around the face than lace, so start with a lace blouse (or organza blouse trimmed with lace) with a wide scoop-neck, off-the-shoulder neckline. Team it with a cream-color moiré skirt. Keep the whole outfit in cream—it's your favorite color, and so feminine. Cream velvet ribbon, cream-color porcelain jewelry instead of the usual real gold, a cream brocade open-toed pump. Sheer cream stockings. Soft pastel makeup—a particularly good choice because many women tend to put on more and more makeup with the years. Less looks younger.

Classic → Sexy

Here, Classic's familiar suit is suddenly sexy in its cling and bareness. Even at that, Classic's subtlety is in command: She crosses over to Sexy not by removing her jacket, but by the mere implication of bareness.

Classic → Sexy

The Situation: You're a reporter going to the Cannes Film Festival—for business and pleasure.

The Problem: You want to look dynamite—maybe not even look American! Sexy Italian is what you'd love to try.

The Crossover Solution: You're going to do business, but you want to be a part of the international jet set. Wear your highest styled suit, but this time without its blouse. Only the most beautiful bare lace camisole should peek out suggestively from underneath the tailored jacket. No distraction of jewelry at your bare low neckline, just strong dangling earrings (probably your first pair).

Exotic → Sporty

The Situation: You're going through Africa on safari.

The Problem: How to retain your Exotic signature—and sense of humor—in primitive surroundings without slowing down the whole safari.

The Crossover Solution: Walking shorts, and an oversized T-shirt—tied in a knot at one side—in cool, comfortable fabrics. The T-shirt could flaunt the message "Save Grand Central Station." On your feet, hiking boots instead of Sporty's sneakers, and layered socks in fun colors.

Exotic → Classic

The Situation: You're a savvy entrepreneur asked to give a speech on how to run a small business.

The Problem: How to look approachable, as well as highly competent and striking, while getting your audience to concentrate on what you're saying, not on how you look.

The Crossover Solution: Wear a gabardine suit in taupe, with a straight skirt, mid-calf length with a high slit. (The long lines of your suit will say Exotic, even though the fabric and color are Classic's.) The jacket is a loose, open-front kimono style, straight and unlined, with rounded shoulders and a simple jewel neckline. Add taupe suede pumps;

Exotic → Arty

Here, Exotic lets go of "stark" to cross over to Arty at its most sophisticated—mixing fabrics, layers, colors, patterns, and textures to the limit.

sheer, slightly textured, taupe hose; a shell blouse in eggplant silk; and a large Byzantine gold pin—the one strong jewelry focus to underline your Exotic look. Keep makeup toned down and hairdo eased up so the overall look is less severe and stylized, more approachable.

Exotic → Arty

The Situation: You're invited to a gala museum opening. The painter is your date, and he's always criticized you as dressing too severely and not looking like fun.

The Problem: You've got to let go of "stark," but you have to maintain drama or you won't stand out in the crowd.

The Crossover Solution: Wear your own simple backdrop of a jumpsuit and top it with the most opulent printed coat and contrasting scarves. Only you could carry off Arty at its most sophisticated and not get lost in the mixed fabrics, layers, colors, patterns, and textures. Walk in with a light swinging step that says you've done it.

Exotic → Feminine

The Situation: You're going to meet your fiancé's parents for the first time.

The Problem: Parents always love femininity. Yet Exotic to Feminine is the most difficult switch because it's the very antithesis of your basic nature, which is strength and style.

The Crossover Solution: A dusty rose bias-cut cashmere skirt and a matching over-sweater with a wide jewel neck and roll-up sleeves. The top is worn over the skirt and belted in at the waist, gathered in a draped yoke over the hips. The rose color and the soft texture of cashmere say feminine. Silver pumps and an antique silver necklace finish the look. Instead of wearing your hair up, wear it down, with combs. Even your makeup is toned down, for feminine softness.

Exotic → Sexy

The Situation: You're taking a course in twentieth-century drama and you've got a crush on your professor.

The Problem: You'd like to pique his interest with more than your term paper.

The Crossover Solution: You wear a skimpy little hot, sultry 1940s flower print rayon dress with jewel neck, big shoulders, short puff sleeves, and buttons from neck to hem. The rayon shows off your figure, and you unbutton a few buttons at the bottom to show off your legs. Plastic, colored earrings, your hair full and tousled, ankle-strap sandals, no stockings, and toenails polished red complete the picture.

Arty → Sporty

The Situation: The new man in your life plays a lot of serious tennis, and you feel you owe him some serious spectating.

The Problem: Everyone looks so Preppy, you'll stand out in a way you might prefer not to, unless you adopt a more expected, conventional look for sports.

The Crossover Solution: Wear Sporty's sweater and skirt, only in your color of olive and in your length of long. Pull the outfit together with a long, knotted charcoal gauze scarf around your neck. It's as close to the expected as an Arty can look. It's adding funk to conventionality, so right you could go to the races at Ascot in it.

Arty → Classic

The Situation: You've just been elected chairwoman of the Save-the-Trees Committee in your borough.

The Problem: You have to raise money; not by marching as you've done so often, but by impressing some heavy contributors.

The Crossover Solution: You need Immediate Classic—structure and body. Try Classic's wool challis skirt in the off-color foulard pattern of eggplant and taupe. Such color and texture are comfortable for Arty, and they give your look strength and importance, since they are more familiarly conventional than your usual. Add a classic, long-sleeved, cream silk blouse worn on the outside and belted, and finish with a large wool shawl in a compatible print. It's Arty softened—and yet classically Classic.

Arty → Sporty

Arty's way of crossing over to Sporty is to take Sporty's uniform of sweater and skirt and *make each piece long*—long enough to be Arty. The bigger-than-usual proportions make funk out of conventionality.

Arty → Exotic

The Situation: You're celebrating one of the Big birthdays (never mind which one).

The Problem: It's time to show you've grown up at last.

The Crossover Solution: For Arty, Exotic is overnight grown-up. Just crossing over into Exotic is enough to bring it off. The main trick is to simplify: go from a big look—like a menswear jacket—to the strong, stylized look of a magenta-and-black suede dress, mid-calf in length. Keep your own black boots, sleek down your hair, and you've got it: Arty as sophisticated Exotic.

Arty → Feminine

The Situation: An architect you work with has asked you out.

The Problem: How do you introduce the softness of a social, personal relationship into what has, up to now, been strictly business give-and-take?

The Crossover Solution: Do it with a big soft ribbed sweater in mauve (the closest thing to pink) over matching trumpet skirt (the closest thing to a ruffle, something he's never seen you in). The outfit is not too fussy or frilly, but still textured enough for your taste. Instead of your beloved boots, sheer gray stockings and gray low-heeled pumps. Finish with soft hair, soft makeup, and a string of pearls.

Arty → Sexy

The Situation: You have a Class Reunion coming up—and fond memories of certain class members (now men!) who are still said to be single.

The Problem: If Arty didn't get them then, maybe Sexy will now—but you need to change to Sexy so cleverly that they'll still remember Arty.

The Crossover Solution: Wear a low-neck angora sweater, belted tight over a straight skirt. (You're halfway there.) Choose the outfit in your favorite smoky color, purple. De-frizz your hair into a soft wave; do a careful makeup job with eyeshadow, blush, and lipstick; and make your entrance in the highest heels you can wear without falling over.

Feminine → Sporty

The Situation: It's parents' visiting day at school. You're a nursery school teacher around little kids all the time, down on your hands and knees as much as you're up on your feet.

The Problem: You want to be comfortable but still look professional to the parents.

The Crossover Solution: Instead of the usual floral skirt, wear washable crisp cotton pants and a soft cotton blouse with a little embroidered collar. For layering, add Sporty's easy unlined jacket, but in your flower print and in soft colors.

Push up the sleeves as Sporty would and you're ready for Parents' Day—feminine, practical, and even, in light of the work, professional.

Feminine → Classic

The Situation: You own a small chain of dress shops, and you've called a press conference to announce expansion plans into new territory.

The Problem: You want to impress the news people with your status and authority as owner of a highly successful business—with the aim of getting good coverage in their papers.

The Crossover Solution: You appear in a teal wool crepe suit, with a lace jabot at the neckline instead of a blouse; sheer taupe stockings and taupe pumps instead of your usual flats; and accessorize with pearls to continue the soft look. If your hair is very wavy, brush it down with combs to tame it.

Feminine → Exotic

The Situation: You want to sell impressionistic art—and you know there's a job open at a certain gallery.

The Problem: You suspect you always come across as too sweet and soft to get a selling job, so you want to cross over to Exotic to prove you've got the authority the sophisticated job calls for.

The Crossover Solution: Wear a simple white raw silk dress of almost triangular shape with wide shoulders, narrowed-in hemline, and push-up sleeves. Wear strong, simple earrings—possibly a flower, but

Feminine → Sporty

Feminine crosses over to Sporty in one inspired combination: Sporty's pants and blazer and Feminine's beloved flower prints. The floral print is so quintessentially Feminine that even in a tailored blazer with crisp pants, it's her femininity that rules.

bigger and stronger—sheer white stockings and royal blue pumps. The overall effect: stark simplicity that speaks well of your sophistication and understanding of the job.

Feminine → Arty

The Situation: You've run into an old college friend you haven't seen in years—a girl who sings with a small rock group—and you're going out to dinner with her.

The Problem: You want to let her know that you're not so different from her, that you know something about her world of music.

The Crossover Solution: Go Arty for the evening with a poet blouse and wrap skirt (slightly longer than usual) in dusty blue gauze, just a little bit muted. No flower on the blouse, but an interesting belt with small sculptures—shells, animals, stones, and such—hanging from it and dangling earrings with similar embellishments. Shake out your hair for the look of loose fullness and then tie it up with a piece of matching gauze fabric. Complete the outfit with ballet slippers and slightly textured, tinted blue hose or, in a different mood perhaps, no stockings or ballet shoes at all—just tie-up sandals.

Feminine → Sexy

The Situation: After years of dating kindly, protective men you've caught the interest of a much more exciting, but dangerous, kind of man.

The Problem: It looks as if you're in for some real competition from a very sexy friend of yours.

The Crossover Solution: A one-piece jumpsuit in electric blue silk. You won't feel uneasy in it because it's so effortless. You'll be quite covered, so it's not blatant in any way. Tie it with a wide metallic belt in pewter and wear sheer silver stockings with high-heeled open strappy pewter sandals. Leave your top open as low as you dare and invite further attention with truly glamorous earrings, clustered rhinestone flowers for example. Make sure your hair is as full as it can possibly be—you might even put new highlights in it for evening.

Sexy → Sporty

The Situation: You're Sexy—and you have kids.

The Problem: It shouldn't be a surprising combination—given the nature of things—and yet people don't expect it.

The Crossover Solution: Let the world know you're happy with both sides of your life. Wear 1940s drawstring baggy flowered shorts instead of Sporty's usual. Make them trouser walking shorts with belt loops and pair them with a big oversized man's shirt on top, knotted at the waist. Tie up your hair, wear very little makeup (for that scrubbed look), skip the jewelry, and wear sandals. You're downplaying your curves, but nobody is misled.

Sexy → Classic

The Situation: You're changing jobs and you have an interview with a head-hunter.

The Problem: How to keep his attention riveted on your qualifications instead of your measurements.

The Crossover Solution: Wear a straight skirt of gabardine, a little longer than usual; a cream silk blouse; and a little navy wool crepe jacket that ties at the waist. Keep your jewelry accents down to a stickpin on your lapel and simple gold earrings close to your face (omit anything dangling). Finish with natural sheer stockings and navy pumps. You're in the traditional, acceptable working "uniform." And, quite rightly, you feel like a million dollars.

Sexy → Exotic

The Situation: The Opera Society is giving its annual fund-raising dinner.

The Problem: You want to look strikingly exotic and creative on this occasion, not sexy.

The Crossover Solution: Wear your black wool jersey, buttoned up to the neck and belted low on the hip with metal. Add a black velvet cape and pewter pumps. Finish with jeweled metallic earrings—and that does it! You'll look exciting, chic, and *all covered up.*

Sexy → Arty

Sexy crosses over to Arty with fringes, ethnic jewelry, textured gauze, and wrapped sandals. Such borrowings from Arty can make her look much more relaxed and nonchalant, but not one bit less Sexy. *That's* in her very blood and bones.

Sexy → Arty

The Situation: You're taking classes in jewelry design.

The Problem: Everybody around you is very Arty looking, and you want to contribute your share of that look.

The Crossover Solution: Wear a fringed gauze dress for an instant look of relaxed nonchalance. Finish with Arty's tie-up sandals. And, of course, show your creativity with an important display of jewelry.

Sexy → Feminine

The Situation: Your parents are coming to New York; it's the first time they'll be seeing you on your home turf in five years.

The Problem: You have to tone down Sexy to Feminine for the duration of their stay.

The Crossover Solution: Wear a mauve sweater-dress with a big full top and a gored flared skirt, mid-calf in length. Choose pale gray sheer stockings with a gray medium-heeled sandal and pearl earrings. Result: "instant decent."

Fantasy Crossover

Quite apart from whether anything in your life demands a crossover, if you've always fantasized about being another image-type, experiment and get it out of your system—or into your life. Buy a few items of clothing that are soft and feminine—in pale apricot, say—and try to integrate that blouse or sweater into your Sporty-Casual wardrobe. Today's designers have approved all sorts of combinations that would have been unthinkable in years past—even delicate lace with gutsy tweed—making it easier to achieve the Fantasy Crossover. The most sophisticated Crossover is when you understand that each type *can evoke a different response.* And you're skilled enough to use the art of Crossover to get the result you want—even for only a specific occasion.

Natural Crossover

Certain image-types seem to fall into natural pairs—Exotic-Dramatic Creative can easily turn into Arty-Offbeat for a more relaxed look. If you feel thoroughly yourself as a Sporty-Casual, it's a smooth and natural shift to go into Classic-Elegant on your job. If you're a Classic-Elegant by day, it's not a big jump to go Exotic for the evening. (It's more like a glide.) And it's almost inevitable that Feminine-Romantic can shade into Sexy-Alluring by cocktail time without feeling the least bit un-comfortable.

If we all compared notes, we'd find that every image-type ap-proaches her crossover in the smallest possible steps. You're Sporty-Casual, but don't you sometimes sneak a glance at Cartier watches? Don't you find yourself running your hand over the silk blouses in your favorite department store? You've even tried to let your hair grow a bit longer——you gave up and cut it because you didn't know how to handle it. Somewhere down deep you wish you could be Classic-Elegant, but you don't know how to try it or where to start. You're nervous about the commitment you're sure it will take. But one day, you're intrigued enough to cross over with a cream silk shirt——and worry about the clean-ing later.

One-Step-at-a-Time Crossover

As a Classic-Elegant, *your* first small step toward crossing over is getting bored. (You wouldn't dream of telling anyone.) You'd love to borrow something unboring so you won't look the same to yourself all the time. Besides, it would be such fun to shake everyone up for once. You eye the big wide belts in the strong, insistent colors. You try on bold, ex-otic earrings and ankle-strap shoes, and you like the effect. Just a touch, of course. But just one touch of exotica is crossover enough for now. So you buy a wide hip belt designed by someone you've never heard of, but you opt for the natural color over bright green——after all, you did com-mit for just one step.

And you, Exotic-Dramatic that you are, who would ever guess you get exhausted by being "on" all the time? Planning and innovating and being ahead of the pack is more tiring than you'd ever let on. You cast an envious eye at far-out Arty (even farther out than you!). Not so much for her look, as for the comfort and freedom of not having to be perfect. You mutter about things like leather and cutting your hair real short. Short hair! That's the crossover: a dramatic short haircut. However, caution prevails: It's still highly stylized and all one color. Even for Exotic, cross-overs should be one step at a time.

If you're an Arty-Offbeat, you have a different problem. You've been Arty for so long you almost don't know there's any other way, but sometimes you feel your look is too much of a hodge-podge. You'd like to exchange the dangling earrings, the Turkish beads, and the Haitian belt for something more striking, less ethnic. You're attracted by Exotic's lack of clutter, clean lines, and strong simple message. You take your first step in that direction by replacing your three small necklaces with one bold one, and suddenly you notice people's eyes are drawn to your face. So let it happen——you'll worry about makeup next month.

And you, are you a Feminine-Romantic with secret yearnings? Do you feel as if you're still wearing Mary Janes and your personality hasn't changed since you were twelve? Sexy looks so alluring. Maybe a little too grown-up for your taste, but you don't have to borrow more than a straight skirt to get the effect you want. That's all it takes, the skirt doesn't even have to have a slit.

You may be a Sexy-Alluring in the mood for change. There are times you're tired of being a threat when in your heart you know you're not. You long for a bit of Feminine-Romantic softness just to give a little play to a different part of your inner self—though not going too far, of course, just with a touch or two. How to do it? You can't give up red, or slits. Can't stand pink. Yet a soft ruffle at the bosom has a certain appeal. There's something demure about it, no matter how low it is. And why not go all the way? Make it dusty rose! What if it does take a hunk an extra twenty seconds to notice you.

Many women have asked, "But what if you're a different person on the inside from what you seem on the outside?" You may be surprised to hear that doesn't happen as much as you might think. If it were really so, inconsistencies in your presentation would have been showing up for a long time. Whenever a client says she wants to look like a totally different image-type, it's usually because she hasn't understood her image parameters correctly. If, for instance, you've always been seen by others as Arty-Offbeat, but you claim you're really a Classic-Elegant at heart, you have to analyze why that type has never surfaced in your style.

Switching to another image-type can be lots of fun—for you *and* the people in your life. But it does take a substantial investment. If the switch is going to be effective, you have to support it wholeheartedly with

Attitude Crossover

the right makeup, hairdo, and accessories. (However, how you wear your old outfit can sometimes make the change even more than a new outfit: rolling up your pants-leg to be more Sporty, pulling your hair off your face with a strip of lace to be more Feminine, cinching in your waist to be more Sexy.)

Switching takes a lot more time and effort, there's no doubt about it, but it also delivers a lot *for* that time and effort. If you're not sure, you can do it in easy steps. The most elementary ways to test out a new image-type is through accessories. Try switching to the accessories of

Accessory Crossover

another image-type with one of your plainest outfits; this way there won't be too much of a contrast between your core type and the new additions. If you don't feel comfortable with them, drop the experiment. If you feel good when you wear them, it's a clue that you can go further. And accessories don't have to cost a lot.

If there's a part of you that gets a certain secret delight in shaking people up, making them really look at you . . . nothing does it like change. If you practice switching regularly—across the board with pieces of clothing and accessories—you'll never find yourself in a rut.

To give yourself every chance to succeed, rehearse privately. Don't go public on your first attempt. Wear the new accessories when you're with your husband or a close friend. If you're a Sexy who wants to be Classic, start small—with colors, rather than with silhouette. Try a soft beige dress, or a quiet cream, instead of your bright red or electric blue. If you feel better about yourself you'll know right away. And, of course, you can still have your sexy hairdo and makeup with the new Classic clothes. Or say you're a Feminine who'd like to try Sexy. Get rid of baby-doll prints and go bold—in jewelry, color, or line. Avoid your beloved pastels, try slinkier, shinier fabrics. If you're trying satin, make it a small step so you can carry it off. Keep to your favorite pink or peach, but because it's *satin* pink or peach, it won't look so little-girl sweet.

Always keep in mind that personality is always stronger than body. If you're a wholesome Preppy type, Arty-Offbeat just isn't going to work for you. You'll know—almost as quickly as your public will—when you're wearing something that conflicts with your true essence. Essence is stronger and will always come through.

On the other hand, you'll be surprised at how much you can do toward overcoming your physical givens. If you have a boyish body—angular and lean—and you'd like to project a feminine, even sexy, image, it's not as hard as you might think. You can do it, not with ruffles and flounces, but with feminine fabrics and colors. Do it with a change of hairdo, a longer, freer style. You can do it by wearing a wider waistband to define your body, shorts that are pleated and shorter instead of plain and longer, and padding around in ballet slippers instead of your usual loafers. Each change may seem almost insignificant, but one on one on one, they can add up to a striking difference. And yet, because they don't attempt to contradict your essence, they move you into an image closer to the one you'd really like to have.

In fashion, as in style, as in life, the first principle remains the same: Know thyself. Know the core of you and you can't go wrong. Once you know that, you can branch out and enjoy the adventure that life should be. Take yourself places—in mind and body and experience—that you were always curious to know, eager to taste, willing to take a chance on. You may discover other selves you never knew were there, and your life will be all the richer for it. Finally, you can say, "It's me. *All* of me!"

9

CONCLUSION: EVERY IMAGE-TYPE IS EXCITING

The inspiration for this book, as with my two previous books, evolved out of the needs of my clients. The more clients I've had, the longer I've worked with them, and the more I've traveled the country, the more I have come to realize that at bottom all women share the same fashion problem.

They don't understand what type they are at the core, and even if they do recognize their type, they often want to be some other, more exciting type. They never see their own potential in reality.

The happy fact is, *every* type is exciting if a woman knows how to express herself to the fullest. In style, as in life, self-acceptance is the first step toward happiness. It has been said that the state of grace is not so much having what you want, as wanting what you have. In the same way, when it comes to personal style, the real triumph comes not so much from being what you like, but liking what you are. I hope this book makes you realize how interesting, how magnetic, your type can be—and how much easier life is if you understand that. It will change the very way you feel about yourself, no longer helpless and vulnerable but confident and sure, because at last you're in complete control of the way you come across to other people.

Once you grasp who you are at the core, you can be as experimental and adventurous as you want. Then, when you try things, you'll discover for the first time that the trying is fun—not a desperate search for self-definition. You're not a slave to fashion hype, a victim of the media. You know how to make fashion work for you.

For a long time now, the "rules" have been flouted, ignored, broken. Handed down by self-styled "experts," or commanded by the dictates of society, "rules" kept women constantly off-balance . . . caught between what they were told they should wear and what they wanted to wear. No wonder so many women felt there had to be a better way.

Dressing has become a totally different art. When today's woman chooses her clothes, it's not to prove she's up on the latest style. (There's something a little old-fashioned about the very thought!) The high-speed life she lives, and the wide range of her activities and responsibilities call for the most intelligent use of all her energies. Today's woman wants her clothes to project not just her sense of style, but her style of life. That's not only the more important message, it's the truer one.

Today, everyone can wear anything anywhere. There are no strict dress codes anymore. You've seen how six different types can attend the same function, at the same time, among the same people—and look so different, so individual, so right. *Because they stay within the parameters of their own image-type.* You will always look right—even in a cross-over—if you preserve your own integrity. That's the only criterion that matters: Is this—this skirt, this jacket, this necklace, this blouse, this dress—*right for you?* Does it say who you are as clearly and authentically as your voice, your smile, your eyes? If it does, you will look fine wherever you are. In today's changing world, the truly interesting woman is the woman who can change and change and change to keep up with today's multifaceted life-styles—and still stay true to herself.

This book aims to help you do that, not by giving you a fashion formula, but by coaching you in a thought process. Once you have that down, I guarantee you'll experience a kind of freedom and confidence that will enhance every other area of your life.

Anthony Loew

About the Authors

Emily Cho's previous books, *Looking Terrific* and *Looking, Working, Living Terrific 24 Hours a Day* changed the way women approached fashion. IT'S YOU, her third and most innovative book, blends confidence, energy and flair with individual style.

Emily Cho is the founder of New Image, a consulting service based in New York. She lives with her husband and two daughters in Manhattan.

Neila Fisher, Emily's partner in New Image, is married and has three sons.

Hermine Lueders is a freelance writer and editor with a husband, three daughters, and a son.